Solving Math Problems in American History

BY
DON BLATTNER AND MYRL SHIREMAN

COPYRIGHT © 2005 Mark Twain Media, Inc.

ISBN 1-58037-316-X

Printing No. D04000

Mark Twain Media, Inc., Publishers
Distributed by Carson-Dellosa Publishing Company, Inc.

Revised/Original title: *Math in American History*

Table of Contents

Table of Contents (cont.)

Introduction

This activity book incorporates aspects of American history and mathematics to reveal a better understanding of the richness of our American heritage. The book is divided into two very distinct parts.

In the first part of the book the growth of the young nation from thirteen independent colonies into a nation of many states is emphasized. During this early period, the nation was basically self-sufficient.

The economy was primarily based on agriculture. Except for the plantations of the South, which produced cotton, tobacco, and other crops for export, farmers mainly produced food for their own families. Any crops produced beyond those needed for family use were exchanged for goods the farmer needed. There was little need for the exchange of money. In this early period most businesses were small, and there was a personal relationship between the owner and his workers. Many of the workers were journeymen learning skills they would later use as owners of their own businesses.

The second part of the book covers the period from 1860 to the present when there were many changes in the nation and its economy. The nation continued to grow and expand. Farmers began producing crops to sell for income. Large factories and companies became commonplace. Unskilled workers began to move to the cities to work in the factories and companies.

As industry grew, the quest for profit became the guiding factor in business. Factory and business owners were no longer connected with the hundreds or thousands of people who worked for them. Churning out the most product at the least expense became the goal.

The government allowed businesses to run without any interference for decades, but new policies to regulate and control businesses were begun in the late 1800s. New laws began to regulate monopolies, workers' wages, and safety.

Inventions throughout the course of American history have changed the way people work and live. This book will explore some of those inventions and their impacts on our society.

In all aspects of American history covered in this book, connections with underlying mathematical concepts are explored. Students will gain an understanding of the math skills needed to be successful in a variety of pursuits including farming, building houses, shopping for supplies, working in a factory, and running a business.

The Thirteen Colonies

America had its beginning in the 1600s when Europeans began to arrive in the New World. In 1607, what is now Jamestown, Virginia, was settled. This was the beginning of the colonization period in American history.

Settlers came to this country for many reasons. Some were the victims of religious persecution in the Old World, and some did not like the government of the country in which they had been living. Still others felt the New World would provide them with wealth. What all of the colonists found, however, was a very hard life. The winters were severe and there was little food along the coast where the first colonists settled. Many of the settlers did not survive even one year.

As a means of supporting themselves, some of the settlers grew tobacco, which they sent to England in exchange for food, supplies, clothing, and furniture. Over a period of years, tobacco farmers prospered, and word of their success got back to Europe. This encouraged more settlers to come to Virginia, the Carolinas, and Maryland to make their fortune growing tobacco.

In 1620 the Pilgrims, who came to America for religious freedom, arrived in the New World on their ship, the Mayflower. They called their settlement Plymouth. In 1623 the first Dutch people arrived in America and settled on Long Island and along the Hudson River in present-day New York State. In 1630 the Puritans arrived from England and settled in what is now Boston. Once these small areas were settled, the population began to grow rapidly. By 1640 there were over 12,500 European settlers in Massachusetts, and by 1660 other colonies were established along the east coast. The colonies continued to grow, and the population of the nation, now known as America, hasn't stopped growing since the first settlers arrived.

Below are the estimated population figures for the thirteen original colonies.

ESTIMATED POPULATIONS OF THE THIRTEEN COLONIES

	1660	1700	1740	1780
Connecticut	8,000	26,000	90,000	207,000
Delaware	500	2,500	20,000	45,000
Georgia	*	*	2,000	56,000
Maryland	8,000	30,000	116,000	245,000
Massachusetts	22,000	56,000	152,000	269,000
New Hampshire	1,500	5,000	23,000	88,000
New Jersey	*	14,000	51,000	140,000
New York	5,000	19,000	64,000	211,000
North Carolina	1,000	11,000	52,000	270,000
Pennsylvania	*	18,000	86,000	327,000
Rhode Island	1,500	6,000	25,000	53,000
South Carolina	*	6,000	45,000	180,000
Virginia	27,000	59,000	180,000	538,000

* Population of less than 500 settlers

Name _____ Date _____

EXERCISE 1: POPULATION IN EARLY AMERICA

The chart on the previous page gives the population for each of the thirteen colonies in the years between 1660 and 1780. Figure the amount of population increase and the percentage of increase for each state for each 40-year period.

EXAMPLE

Find the population increase and percentage of increase for Connecticut between 1660 and 1700.

Step 1: In order to find the increase, subtract Connecticut's population in 1660 from its population in 1700.

$$26,000 - 8,000 = 18,000$$

Step 2: In order to find the percentage of increase, divide the increase by the population of 1660.

$$18,000 \div 8,000 = 2.25$$

Step 3: Move the decimal two places to the right, and add a percent sign.

$$2.25 = 225\%.$$

Connecticut's population increased 225% between 1660 and 1780.

	1660 to 1700		1700 to 1740		1740 to 1780		1660 to 1780	
	Increase	Percentage of Increase	Increase	Percentage of Increase	Increase	Percentage of Increase	Increase	Percentage of Increase
CT	<u>18,000</u>	<u>225%</u>	_____	_____	_____	_____	_____	_____
DE	_____	_____	_____	_____	_____	_____	_____	_____
GA	xxxxxx	xxxxxx	xxxxxx	xxxxxx	_____	_____	xxxxxx	xxxxxx
MD	_____	_____	_____	_____	_____	_____	_____	_____
MA	_____	_____	_____	_____	_____	_____	_____	_____
NH	_____	_____	_____	_____	_____	_____	_____	_____
NJ	xxxxxx	xxxxxx	_____	_____	_____	_____	xxxxxx	xxxxxx
NY	_____	_____	_____	_____	_____	_____	_____	_____
NC	_____	_____	_____	_____	_____	_____	_____	_____
PA	xxxxxx	xxxxxx	_____	_____	_____	_____	xxxxxx	xxxxxx
RI	_____	_____	_____	_____	_____	_____	_____	_____
SC	xxxxxx	xxxxxx	_____	_____	_____	_____	xxxxxx	xxxxxx
VA	_____	_____	_____	_____	_____	_____	_____	_____

Name_____ Date _____

EXERCISE 1: POPULATION IN EARLY AMERICA (CONTINUED)

Answer the following questions based on the information in the chart you completed on the previous page.

1. Which state had the greatest percentage of increase between 1660 and 1700?

_____

2. Which state had the smallest percentage of increase between 1660 and 1700?

_____

3. Which state had the greatest amount of increase between 1660 and 1700?

_____

4. Which state had the smallest amount of increase between 1660 and 1700?

_____

5. Which state had the greatest percentage of increase between 1700 and 1740?

_____

6. Which state had the smallest percentage of increase between 1700 and 1740?

_____

7. Which state had the greatest amount of increase between 1700 and 1740?

_____

8. Which state had the smallest amount of increase between 1700 and 1740?

_____

9. Which state had the greatest percentage of increase between 1740 and 1780?

_____

10. Which state had the smallest percentage of increase between 1740 and 1780?

_____

11. Which state had the greatest amount of increase between 1740 and 1780?

_____

12. Which state had the smallest amount of increase between 1740 and 1780?

_____

Milestones and Roman Numerals

Postage in the colonial period was charged by the mile. The main problem with this method was that there were no accurate measurements between all of the points to which a letter could be mailed. The postman often needed to estimate the distance he actually carried the letter. If the postman had to hike over rough, hilly terrain, he might overestimate the distance he actually traveled and charge more for the letter. It was important, therefore, to devise some method of measuring distances so that people would be charged fairly.

The method chosen was the erection of **milestones**. When people use the term *milestone* today, they are usually referring to an important event in one's life. A graduation, a wedding, the birth of a child, or a retirement is often called a milestone, because each of these is an event that people will likely remember the date of for years. In colonial times, however, milestones were real stones that marked miles to a city. Milestones varied in appearance, but many were made of granite and had letters and numerals chiseled in them. The initial at the top of the milestone indicated a city, and the numerals indicated the miles to the city. The numerals indicating mileage were often written as Roman numerals. Finally, a letter was included that told the post rider what type of measuring system was being used.

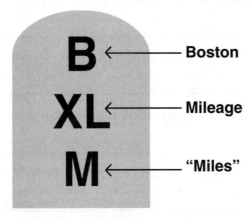

In order to understand the mileage written on milestones, postmen and travelers needed to understand the Roman numeral system. Developed several centuries B.C., the Roman numeral numbering system is a simple system to understand. Here are the symbols used for writing Roman numerals:

I = 1   V = 5   X = 10   L = 50   C = 100   D = 500   M = 1,000

Here is a chart of the values of Roman numerals.

Roman Numerals	I	II	III	IV	V	VI	VII	VIII	IX	X
Arabic Numbers	1	2	3	4	5	6	7	8	9	10

Roman Numerals	X	XX	XXX	XL	L	LX	LXX	LXXX	XC	C
Arabic Numbers	10	20	30	40	50	60	70	80	90	100

Name _____ Date _____

EXERCISE 2: ROMAN NUMERALS

Roman numerals may be used in various combinations in order to enable a person to write any number. For example, the number 521 would be expressed as a Roman numeral in the following way: DXXI.

There are three important rules to remember when writing or reading Roman numerals.

Rule 1: The values of the symbols are read from left to right. When the symbols are in order from greatest to least value from left to right, they are to be added together to get the total value of the numeral. The symbol with the highest value is at the left, the symbol with the second highest value is just to the right of that symbol, and the next highest value is just to the right, and so on.

EXAMPLE

The numerals III, XX, C, which might represent the number 123, would be arranged in the following order: CXXIII. C (100) would be placed first since it has the highest value, and then the other numerals, XX (20) and III (3), would follow in decreasing value.

Place the following numerals in order of greatest to least value:

1. DCC, I, XXX, M _____   2. III, D,V _____

3. C, II, L _____   4. LX, II, C _____

5. C, D, M, X, I_____   6. D, M, X, II _____

Rule 2: When a Roman numeral that is of the same value or of less value comes after another Roman numeral, add their values.

EXAMPLE

XX III (20 + 3 = 23)   M D C IV (1000 + 500 + 100 + 4 = 1604)
L XXX VI (50 + 30 + 6 = 86)   D L III (500 + 50 + 3 = 553)

Follow Rule 2 in order to change the following Roman numerals into Arabic numbers:

7. DC _____   8. XI _____   9. LXIII _____

10. XXVI _____   11. MDLXI _____   12. DCLXXII _____

Name_____ Date _____

EXERCISE 2: ROMAN NUMERALS (CONTINUED)

Rule 3: When a Roman numeral of smaller value comes before another Roman numeral of larger value, subtract the smaller from the larger.

EXAMPLE

IX (10 - 1 = 9)   IV (5 - 1 = 4)   CD (500 - 100 = 400)   XL (50 - 10 = 40)

CM IV (1,000 - 100 = 900; 5 - 1 = 4; 900 + 4 = 904)

Follow Rule 3 in order to change the following Roman numerals into Arabic numerals:

13. CM _____   14. CD _____   15. XC _____

16. CD IV _____   17. CD IX _____   18. XL IV _____

Fill in the missing blanks.

	Arabic Numeral	Roman Numeral		Arabic Numeral	Roman Numeral
19.	34	_____	31.	17	_____
20.	19	_____	32.	23	_____
21.	7	_____	33.	318	_____
22.	_____	XXVI	34.	490	_____
23.	_____	CLXII	35.	_____	MDC
24.	_____	LX	36.	_____	MDCCXX
25.	_____	XXXIX	37.	_____	CCCXXXVI
26.	_____	XXVII	38.	_____	MDCCCLX
27.	_____	CCL	39.	_____	DCXXXIII
28.	45	_____	40.	_____	MDCCCXXVI
29.	69	_____	41.	_____	MDXII
30.	54	_____	42.	_____	MCDLXXXIV

Disadvantages of the Roman Numeral System

The Roman numeral system is very easy to understand. On the other hand, the simplicity of the system limits its usefulness. There are four main problems with using Roman numerals as a numbering system:

1. The system does not use a zero.

2. The system does not use the concept of place value—the idea that the place or position of a digit decides its value.

3. The numeral can become very long (MMDCCLXXXVIII).

4. While adding and subtracting with Roman numerals is relatively easy, it is impossible to multiply or divide using this system. There are some problems below. Just for fun, solve them.

ADD   **SUBTRACT**

ADD	SUBTRACT
MD	MDCCXXXVII
CCC	DC XX I
L	
XX	
IV	

Obviously the cumbersome aspect of the Roman numeral system is one of the main reasons that it has been replaced by the Arabic system. However, it is important to understand the Roman numeral system since it is an important part of our cultural past and is still used as an artistic method of recording dates and other numbers.

Homesteading on the Prairie

Early houses on the prairie were very crude. They were often rough log cabins with plank roofs and generally consisted of one room and a sleeping loft for the children. The cabins were small, dirty, drab, and barely kept out the snow, rain, and wind.

Clearing the land was the first job pioneers faced when they selected a spot to build their home. If they selected a spot where there were many trees, the trees had to be cleared from the location. Fortunately, those trees were an excellent material to use for building the home. This is why we think of log cabins when we think of the pioneers. The homesteaders not only needed to clear the land, they also needed to determine the number, size, and length of the logs they needed to build the walls of the cabin, as well as the number of shingles they would need to cover the roof.

After a homesteader decided on the location of his cabin, he would invite his neighbors to help him build it. The homesteader supplied food and drink, and the event was considered a social occasion for the whole community. While the men labored building the cabin with hand tools, the women prepared food. Everyone worked all day and celebrated all night. The neighbors stayed several days until the house was completed.

Building the home was a fairly routine affair. The workers selected trees about ten inches thick, chopped them down, and then cut the logs to the desired lengths. Two large logs laid parallel to each other ran the length of the house and served as the base logs. The men then rolled the logs for the walls up on inclined poles and stacked them two at a time. Two were stacked on the sides, and then two were stacked on the ends until the walls were finished. The ends of these logs were notched so that the logs of one wall would be locked to the logs of the intersecting wall where they met. While most of the earlier cabins had dirt floors, later the men split logs in half and placed these half logs on the foundation logs with their flat sides up so that the occupants could have the luxury of a wooden floor.

The roofs were made of planks called clapboards. Clapboard shingles were made from logs that were cut into three-foot lengths. The three foot logs were placed on end. Then, using a tool with a long, sharp blade, the men split planks about one inch thick from the log. These planks, called clapboards, were placed on the roof in an overlapping pattern in order to keep the rain out. Nails were generally not used in the roofs, so the clapboard shingles were held in place by long poles that ran the length of the house and were secured at the ends.

The openings for the fireplace and the door were cut with a saw, and planks framed the doorway and the fireplace so that the logs would not sag. Early cabins were built with no windows in order to protect the homesteaders from Indians. The few cabins that did have windows generally did not have glass in the windows. Instead, they had shutters that could be closed in bad weather and for protection but opened when the weather was pleasant.

The final task in completing the cabin was weatherproofing. Homesteaders did this by filling the spaces between the logs and the cracks around the door and any other openings with a mixture of mud and moss.

After the cabin was finished, there was a housewarming. Everyone who had helped build the cabin attended. There was drinking, dancing, and eating. Building a house was a tough job, but everyone that helped enjoyed themselves.

Name _____ Date _____

EXERCISE 3: HOW MANY LOGS TO BUILD A CABIN?

Figure the number of logs needed to build a house that measures 16 feet x 20 feet. The diameter of the logs is 10 inches. The height of the walls should be as close to 8 feet 5 inches as possible. Only full logs will be used. Figure the number of the logs needed for the walls only. Do not figure the number of logs needed to build the gable of the house. The gable is the triangular section of wall at the end of the pitched roof, or the space between the two slopes of the roof.

1. The number of 16-foot logs needed is _____ .

2. The number of 20-foot logs needed is _____ .

Figure the number of logs needed to build a house that measures 15 feet x 22 feet. The height of the walls should be as close to 9 feet 3 inches as possible. Use full logs only.

3. The number of 15-foot logs needed is _____ .

4. The number of 22-foot logs needed is _____ .

Figure the number of logs needed to build a house that is 14 feet x 30 feet. The height of the walls should be as close to 9 feet 1 inch as possible. Use full logs only.

5. _____ 14-foot logs are needed.

6. _____ 30-foot logs are needed.

Figure the number of logs needed to build a house that is 20 feet x 24 feet. The height of the walls should be as close to 10 feet as possible. Use full logs only.

7. _____ 20-foot logs are needed.

8. _____ 24-foot logs are needed.

Name _____ Date _____

Sod Houses

The kind of timber necessary for log cabins was unavailable in some areas of the plains states. Pioneers who settled in these areas usually built sod houses or dugouts. As the name implies, sod homes were literally constructed from the sod found in the area. Dugouts were built by digging a hole into a hill so that the house was like a cave. The back of the house and most of the sides were actually in the hill, while the front of the house and parts of the sides were made of sod.

Sod houses and dugouts had several advantages over log cabins. The thick sod acted as the insulation. When the weather was very cold, a small fire was able to heat the home, and the settlers stayed warm. When the weather was hot, the home remained cool. It was almost like living in a cave. There were some disadvantages to these types of homes, however. After all, they were made of earth. When it rained heavily, the house became soggy and leaked. Dugouts presented other problems. A horse and rider or a cow could fall through the ceiling if they happened to be walking on the hill.

The construction of the sod house was quite simple, but a tremendous amount of sod was required. Settlers used a plow to dig the sod several inches deep, and then they cut the sod into two- or three-foot lengths. Sod was very heavy and had to be carried by hand or transported by wheelbarrow or wagon from the field to the house. For this reason the pioneers chose to place the house close to the location where the sod was to be dug. Sod bricks, which were generally two to four inches thick, about 12 inches wide, and approximately 20 inches long, were then stacked to form the walls. Most sod houses consisted of one room that was divided by curtains.

Figuring the amount of sod needed for a house is a little more difficult than figuring the number of logs required for a cabin. It is doubtful that pioneers really sat down to figure the number of cubic feet of sod they would need in order to build their house. They just looked at the sod available and then made a judgment of whether they had enough for the project or not. But for the next exercise we will figure the amount of sod needed for houses of various sizes. The principle of figuring the amount of sod used in a sod house is the same principle used for other construction projects, such as the construction of a brick home.

EXERCISE 4: HOW MUCH SOD IS NEEDED FOR A SOD HOUSE?

EXAMPLE

How much sod is needed for a wall 10 feet high, 1 foot thick, and 16 feet long? The sod you intend to use is 2 inches thick, 12 inches wide, and 20 inches long.

Step 1: Find the number of inches in a cubic foot by multiplying the dimensions of a cubic foot.

12″ x 12″ x 12″ = 1,728 cubic inches in a cubic foot.

Name _____ Date _____

EXERCISE 4: HOW MUCH SOD NEEDED FOR A SOD HOUSE? (CONT.)

Step 2: Find the number of cubic inches in one sod brick by multiplying the dimensions of a sod brick.

2″ x 12″ x 20″ = 480 cubic inches in one sod brick.

Step 3: Find the number of sod bricks you will need for a cubic foot by dividing the number of cubic inches in a cubic foot by the number of cubic inches in a sod brick.

1,728 ÷ 480 = 3.6 sod bricks in a cubic foot.

Step 4: Find the number of cubic feet in the wall by multiplying the dimensions of the wall.

10′ x 1′ x 16′ = 160 cubic feet in the wall.

Step 5: Find the number of sod bricks needed for the wall by dividing the number of cubic feet in the wall by the number of sod bricks in a cubic foot.

160 ÷ 3.6 = 44.4 sod bricks 2 inches thick, 12 inches wide, and 20 inches long would be needed to build a wall 10 feet high, 1 foot thick, and 16 feet long.

For the following problems round your answers off to the nearest whole sod brick.

1. How much sod is needed for a house that is 10 feet high, 1 foot thick, 16 feet long, and 16 feet wide? The sod you intend to use is 2 inches thick, 12 inches wide, and 15 inches long.

_____

2. How much sod is needed for a house that is 12 feet high, 2 feet thick, 18 feet long, and 16 feet wide? The sod you intend to use is 1 inch thick, 24 inches wide, and 22 inches long.

_____

3. How much sod is needed for a house that is 9 feet high, 1.5 feet thick, 20 feet long, and 10 feet wide? The sod you intend to use is 2 inches thick, 18 inches wide, and 15 inches long.

_____

4. How much sod is needed for a house that is 10 feet high, 1 foot thick, 22 feet long, and 16 feet wide? The sod you intend to use is 2 inches thick, 12 inches wide, and 15 inches long.

_____

5. How much sod is needed for a house that is 11 feet high, 2 feet thick, 19 feet long, and 15 feet wide? The sod you intend to use is 2 inches thick, 12 inches wide, and 20 inches long.

_____

Farming in Early America

Early settlers relied on agriculture to survive. The colonists' chief grain crop was Indian maize, or corn, which they learned to grow from the native Americans. Pumpkins, squash, and beans were the only other vegetables that were common in the early colonies. At first wheat did not grow well in the colonies, but by 1641 it began to be established, and soon wheat was a plentiful crop that was being exported. The settlers' diet was supplemented by hunting the wildlife that was abundant in the new land.

Colonists had little livestock at first, since space was scarce on the ships that brought them to America. In addition, for all of its plentiful wildlife, meadows, and forests, America did not have enough of the type of forage plants domestic livestock needed to eat. There was some wild rye and other grasses and plants that livestock could eat in the summer, but these forage plants did not provide enough nutrients for the animals to survive the harsh New England winters. Nevertheless, colonists needed livestock for food and to work the farm, so they planted English forage plants for feed. By the latter part of the seventeenth century, these forage plants were used by most farmers who had livestock.

Farms were small in early America, usually under 200 acres. The work was all done by hand since there were few animals such as horses, mules, or oxen to haul and plow. The head of a family and his sons did all of the work on the family farm, although in some cases a hired hand, indentured servant, or slave was needed to keep the farm operating.

During the eighteenth century farming began to change. Much of the land near the coast was occupied, so the price on the remaining land increased. Wealthy men, hoping to make a profit on the increasing value of the land, began to purchase large tracts of acreage. By 1730 almost all good land located near the coast was either occupied or owned by wealthy investors. They felt that in the future land would cost more and they could sell it for a huge profit. This speculation caused the value of land to rise considerably, making it impossible for small farmers to purchase any. At the same time, the soil began to "wear out." Farmers in the eighteenth century were unaware of modern conservation techniques that farmers know and practice today. As a result of these trends, farmers began to move to the West.

The land between the Appalachian Mountains and the Mississippi River provided a great opportunity for pioneers. The earth was fertile, and crops grew well. One of the challenges homesteaders faced was clearing the land. Once the trees were cut, homesteaders had to contend with the stumps and tree roots. Working with wooden plows made this a formidable task. A man walked behind the plow trying to hold it down as a boy drove the oxen pulling the plow. Once the land was plowed, corn, the primary crop, was planted.

Most farmers also raised swine. In the summer the swine were fed kitchen scraps, and in the winter they were released into the forest. The forest provided a feast for the hogs. Acorns, beechnuts, and other forest morsels enabled the hogs to become huge in a short time. The farmer used most of the swine to feed his own family. Any pork not used by the family could be exported as salt pork.

As labor-saving devices were introduced into agriculture, farmers became more productive. They not only were able to produce enough food to feed their families, but they were also able to sell the livestock and crops they did not need. This enabled American farmers to build better homes, buy more land, and expand their farms.

Name_____ Date _____

EXERCISE 5: FIGURE THE INCOME OF A NINETEENTH CENTURY FARMER

Shown below is a list of items a nineteenth century farmer might have produced and sold. Figure the price he would receive for his crops and livestock. Before you work the problems, you should know that the abbreviation *cwt* stands for hundredweight. In other words, cwt is equal to 100 pounds. You should also be aware that there are 2,000 pounds in a ton.

During one year, a farmer sold the following items. Put the amount he received on the blank next to each item. Round your answer off to the nearest whole cent. Then find the total income for the year.

1. A load of hay weighing 1,875 lbs. at $14.25 per ton _____

2. A lot of straw weighing 9,855 lbs. at $1.23 per ton_____

3. 1,465 lbs. of pork at $4.44 per cwt. _____

4. 9,365 lbs. of hogs at $3.68 per cwt. _____

5. A cow weighing 871 lbs. at 5 ¾¢ per lb. _____

6. 512 bushels of corn at 98¢ per bushel_____

7. 329 bushels of wheat at $1.37 per bushel _____

8. 1,025 bushels of barley at 92 ½¢ per bushel _____

9. 1,112 bushels of oats at 32¢ per bushel_____

10. 57 chickens at 16¢ each _____

11. 112 bushels of potatoes at 69¢ per bushel _____

12. 91 bushels of apples at $1.31 per bushel _____

13. 22 bushels of peaches at $1.67 per bushel _____

14. 102 gallons of milk at 23¢ a gallon _____

15. 232 lbs. of sheep at $4.17 per cwt. _____

16. 57 bushels of grapes at $2.22 per bushel _____

17. 512 dozen eggs at 8 ½¢ per dozen _____

18. 37 pounds of butter at 9 ¼¢ per pound _____

19. Total _____

Dealing With Gross and Net Measurements

When farmers sold their hogs to be sent to packing houses to be turned into hams, bacon, pork chops, and other products, a distinction was made between the **gross** weight of the hogs and the **net** weight of the hogs. The gross weight of the hogs referred to their full weight when the hogs were alive. The net weight referred to the weight of the hogs after they were killed and dressed. A dressed hog is one that has been slaughtered, skinned, cleaned, trimmed, and prepared to be sold to a butcher shop. The distinction between these two weights was important because the price of the hogs was determined by the weight, and the net weight was less than the gross weight. Both the seller and the buyer needed to know which weight was being referred to in order to determine the price of the hog.

The standard difference between the net weight and the gross weight of a hog was $\frac{1}{5}$ or 20 percent. In other words, the net weight of a hog was generally considered to be 20 percent less than its gross weight. Another way of saying it would be that the net weight of a hog was 80 percent of its gross weight. (100% - 20% = 80%)

Example: A hog that weighs 495 pounds gross would weigh approximately 396 pounds net. There are two ways to do this problem. You can multiply the gross weight by 20 percent and then subtract the answer from the gross weight. 495 x 0.20 = 99; 495 - 99 = 396. A simpler and faster method would be to multiply the gross weight by 80 percent, since the net weight is 80 percent of the gross weight. 495 x 0.80 = 396.

The same formula is used in order to find the **gross price** if the **net price** of pork is given. The net price will be the larger price in the formula, since dressed meat costs more per pound than live hogs. The price difference will again be 20 percent.

Example: If the net price of pork is $3.80 cwt, then the gross price is $3.04 (3.80 x 0.80 = 3.04).

Sometimes the farmer knew the net weight of the hogs and needed to find the gross weight. In order to do this, he divided the net weight by 80 percent.

Example: If the net weight of a hog was 396 lbs., then the gross weight would be 495 lbs. (396 ÷ 0.80 = 495.)

The same formula is used in order to find the **net price** of pork if the **gross price** is given.

Example: If the gross price of pork is $3.04, then the net price is $3.80 (3.04 ÷ 0.80 = 3.80).

Name _____ Date _____

EXERCISE 6: FINDING THE GROSS AND NET WEIGHT AND PRICE OF HOGS

In each case below, you are given either the gross or net weight. Find the missing weight using the formulas on the previous page. Round off your answers to the nearest pound.

	Gross Weight	Net Weight
1.	502 lbs.	_____
2.	620 lbs.	_____
3.	_____	408 lbs.
4.	_____	322 lbs.
5.	407 lbs.	_____
6	_____	517 lbs.
7.	614 lbs.	_____
8.	487 lbs.	_____
9.	_____	481 lbs.
10.	_____	527 lbs.

In each case below, you are given either the gross or net price. Find the missing price using the formulas on the previous page. Round off your answer to the nearest whole cent.

	Net Price	Gross Price
11.	$3.45	_____
12.	$4.07	_____
13.	_____	$4.25
14.	$3.98	_____
15.	_____	$4.55
16.	$4.29	_____
17.	$3.87	_____
18.	_____	$4.00
19.	_____	$4.18
20.	_____	$4.57

Mathematics Around The Farm

Farmers used mathematics often. They not only needed to be able to calculate the cost and profit on produce and livestock, they also had to determine the capacities of bins, granaries, corn cribs, wagon beds, and cisterns. They needed to know if they had enough space to store all of the grain they had. They also needed to be able to measure and determine how much hay made a ton.

GRAIN MEASURING

Grain was transported by wagon and was stored in bins and granaries. These containers for grain were rectangular. To figure the amount of grain needed to fill any of these, farmers needed to use the formula to find the volume for a rectangular solid.

Rule: To find the volume of a rectangular solid, multiply the linear measure in length by the linear width and the linear height. The formula is $V = l \times w \times h$.
Sometimes it is simply written $V = lwh$

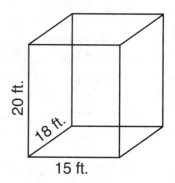

Example: A bin with the dimensions of 20 ft. x 15 ft. x 18 ft. has the capacity of 5,400 cubic feet.
(20 ft. x 15 ft. x 18 ft. = 5,400 cu. ft.)

16

Name _____   Date _____

EXERCISE 7: FIGURING THE CAPACITIES OF GRANARIES, BINS, AND WAGONS

All of your answers in the following problems will be in cubic feet. Round all answers to the nearest whole foot. Find the capacity of a granary:

1. 18 ft. x 16 ft. x 12 ft. = _____

2. 22 ft. x 16 ft. x 14 ft. = _____

3. 25 ft. x 22 ft. x 15 ft. = _____

4. 28 ft. x 26 ft. x 22 ft. = _____

5. 26 ft. x 23 ft. x 21 ft. = _____

6. 20 ft. x 13 ft. x 9 ft. = _____

7. 23 ft. x 12 ft. x 8 ft. = _____

8. 24 ft. x 10 ft. x 7 ft. = _____

9. 19 ft. x 11 ft. x 8 ft. = _____

Find the capacity of a bin:

10. 8.5 ft. x 8 ft. x 8.2 ft. = _____

11. 8.3 ft. x 7.4 ft. x 8.1 ft. = _____

12. 7.2 ft. x 6.9 ft. x 8 ft. = _____

13. 8.1 ft. x 7 ft. x 7.3 ft. = _____

14. 10 ft. x 9.9 ft. x 9.8 ft. = _____

15. 9.7 ft. x 8.8 ft. x 9.6 ft. = _____

16. 12.3 ft. x 7.2 ft. x 7.4 ft. = _____

17. 14.7 ft. x 9.1 ft. x 9.9 ft. = _____

18. 15.1 ft. x 8.6 ft. x 9.5 ft. = _____

Find the capacity of a wagon:

19. 12 ft. x $3\frac{1}{2}$ ft. x $2\frac{1}{2}$ ft. = _____

20. 9 ft. x $4\frac{1}{3}$ ft. x $3\frac{1}{6}$ ft. = _____

21. 11 ft. x $5\frac{1}{8}$ ft. x $3\frac{1}{2}$ ft. = _____

22. 8 ft. x $4\frac{1}{4}$ ft. x $2\frac{1}{16}$ ft. = _____

23. $10\frac{1}{4}$ ft. x $3\frac{1}{8}$ ft. x $2\frac{1}{2}$ ft. = _____

24. $10\frac{1}{2}$ ft. x 8 ft. x $3\frac{1}{2}$ ft. = _____

25. $13\frac{1}{4}$ ft. x $5\frac{1}{8}$ ft. x $3\frac{1}{2}$ ft. = _____

26. $14\frac{1}{6}$ ft. x $6\frac{1}{2}$ ft. x $3\frac{1}{8}$ ft. = _____

Name_____ Date _____

EXERCISE 8: FINDING THE WEIGHTS OF HAYSTACKS

Find the size of a haystack and the approximate weight of the haystack on the following stacks. In order to find the amount of hay, use the formula to find the volume of a rectangular solid, V = lwh. Farmers in this period estimated that 500 cubic feet of well-settled hay or about 700 cubic feet of new-mown hay would weigh about a ton. These, of course, are merely approximations, since two identical stacks of hay would contain different levels of moisture and, consequently, would have different weights. The only accurate way to measure hay would be to weigh it. The problem was that most farmers did not have access to scales, so measuring stacks of hay was often the only method farmers could use to estimate the weight.

Figure the approximate weight of the following stacks of hay. Round off your answers to the nearest whole cubic foot.

	Size in Cubic Feet	Weight in Tons
1. Stack of new-mown hay 10 ft. x 16 ft. x 8 ft.	_____	_____
2. Stack of well-settled hay 12 ft. x 14 ft. x 9 ft.	_____	_____
3. Stack of well-settled hay 17 ft. x 13 ft. x 7 ft.	_____	_____
4. Stack of new-mown hay 10.2 ft. x 16.3 ft. x 8.6 ft.	_____	_____
5. Stack of well-settled hay 12.5 ft. x 14.7 ft. x 9.1 ft.	_____	_____
6. Stack of well-settled hay 17.4 ft. x 13.3 ft. x 7.2 ft.	_____	_____
7. Stack of new-mown hay $10\frac{1}{2}$ ft. x $16\frac{1}{4}$ ft. x $8\frac{1}{2}$ ft.	_____	_____
8. Stack of new-mown hay $10\frac{1}{8}$ ft. x $16\frac{1}{16}$ ft. x $8\frac{1}{12}$ ft.	_____	_____
9. Stack of well-settled hay $12\frac{1}{3}$ ft. x $14\frac{1}{6}$ ft. x $9\frac{1}{9}$ ft.	_____	_____
10. Stack of well-settled hay 16 ft. x 16.5 ft. x 8 ft.	_____	_____

Name _____ Date _____

EXERCISE 9: FINDING THE VOLUMES OF CISTERNS

Early American homes did not have running water. They relied on wells, streams, lakes, and rainwater for their water supplies. If a house was close to a water supply, that is what the settlers used. In fact, the closeness to a water source was one of the primary considerations when people decided where to place their homes.

If the house was placed away from a water source and well water was not available, rainwater was collected and used. Drain pipes were placed on the house and arranged so that the rainwater would flow and be collected in barrels at the side of the house or in **cisterns**, which were underground. Cisterns were similar to wells. The earlier ones were constructed of stone or brick, and the later ones consisted of underground tanks. The difference between cisterns and wells was the source of the water. Wells relied on the underground water table and cisterns stored rainwater for later use.

Builders needed to estimate the capacity required for a cistern and then excavate a hole the appropriate size. Obviously, a large family would need a larger cistern than that of a small family.

The rule used to determine the volume of rainwater a cistern would hold is shown below. Since a cistern is a cylinder, the formula for the volume of a cylinder is used.

Rule: The volume of a cylinder is equal to the area of the base multiplied by the height of the cylinder. (Volume = π x r x r x h or V=πr^2h)

EXAMPLE

What is the volume of a cistern that is 8 feet high and has a radius of 4 feet?

$$V = \pi r^2 h \qquad \text{or} \qquad V = \pi \times r \times r \times h$$
$$V = 3.14 \times 4 \text{ ft.} \times 4 \text{ ft.} \times 8 \text{ ft.}$$
$$V = 401.92 \text{ cubic feet}$$

Listed below are the dimensions for several cisterns. Calculate the number of cubic feet each would hold. Your answers will be in cubic feet.

	Radius of the Base	Height	Volume		Radius of the Base	Height	Volume
1.	8 ft.	12 ft.	_____	2.	7 ft.	14 ft.	_____
3.	4 ft.	11 ft.	_____	4.	6 ft.	13 ft.	_____
5.	5.7 ft.	13.6 ft.	_____	6.	5.2 ft.	9.3 ft.	_____
7.	6.1 ft.	14.5 ft.	_____	8.	$3\frac{1}{2}$ ft.	$8\frac{1}{4}$ ft.	_____
9.	$9\frac{1}{3}$ ft.	$17\frac{1}{6}$ ft.	_____	10.	$8\frac{1}{5}$ ft.	$16\frac{1}{8}$ ft.	_____

Trades in Early America

Colonists and pioneers tried to be as self-sufficient as possible. Someone who is self-sufficient is able to provide all the goods and services he or she needs to survive. These early Americans grew their own food, built their own homes, educated themselves, treated their own illnesses, and even made coffins for their own family members. If there was a job too big for a family, such as building a cabin, or if a man was injured and unable to harvest his crops, the neighbors would pitch in and help. In turn, whenever their neighbors needed help, the favor would be returned.

There were certain things, however, that required special skills or special equipment that the pioneers did not have. In these cases they used the services of craftsmen or tradesmen. There were certain tradesmen who could be found in almost every village. There was always a need for a blacksmith, who was a craftsman that used fire, an anvil, and a hammer to forge and shape iron. There was a cobbler, who made and repaired shoes and boots. There was also a miller, who turned grain into flour. These tradesmen usually did not have enough business to work at their trade full time, so they had to do related jobs in order to earn a livelihood.

Some tradesmen traveled from cabin to cabin in order to provide their services. Tinkers would bring all of their tools and materials on horseback in order to sell tinware and repair pots and other household implements. Peddlers might have more than one horse or even a cart laden down with goods that could either be sold to the pioneers or traded for food or something else. Cobblers brought their cobbler's bench containing leather, nails, tools, and lasts, which were wooden forms shaped like feet. The cobbler would set up shop right in the pioneer's cabin and make or repair shoes for family members. A weaver might advertise that he would be in the village on a certain day and then set up his loom at the inn. A woman who had spun her wool at home would go to the inn and tell the weaver the pattern she wanted. With her yarn, he would weave her cloth.

All of the tradesmen who lived in early America needed to know something about mathematics in order to succeed. They needed to keep records of what was bought and sold. For some, math was used everyday. Some examples are given in the following pages.

The Cooper

Coopers made barrels. In Early America almost everything was packed in barrels. Flour, sugar, crackers, pickles, potatoes, nuts, and cider were just a few of the items packed in barrels. Most barrels were of standard size. For example, if someone bought a barrel of cider, they knew that it contained 31 $\frac{1}{2}$ gallons of cider. If they bought a barrel of flour, they knew it contained 196 pounds of flour.

In the Revolutionary Period, a barrel was not only a container to store goods, it was also a standardized measure. The French were the ones who developed this type of measurement. They wanted a system that would enable them to trade their goods with other countries. Their system used gallons, hogsheads, pipes, and tunnels. This measuring system was the basis of the system that was used in the colonies. A hogshead was a barrel twice the size of the standard barrel. A pipe was the size of two hogsheads, and two pipes were the equivalent of a giant hogshead. A giant hogshead was used to transport tobacco. It was so large that it wasn't carried. An axle was placed through the giant hogshead, and an oxen team pulled the huge barrel filled with tobacco from the field to the wharf.

The cooper made two different kinds of barrels. Wet barrels were used for wine, cider, and other liquids. Dry barrels were not watertight and were used for flour, grain, and similar materials. While most of the barrels were made to standard sizes, a cooper could make barrels of different sizes if a client had a special need. For special orders, coopers needed to be able to determine the capacity of the barrels the client needed in order to build them to the correct specifications. For example, if a store clerk needed 20 barrels that were capable of holding ten gallons of molasses, the cooper needed to know how to figure the capacity of barrels. At other times a store clerk may have given the cooper the dimensions of the barrels he wanted.

In order to figure the volume of a barrel, the cooper used the formula for figuring the volume of a cylinder.

Rule: The volume of a cylinder is equal to the area of the base multiplied by the height of the cylinder. (**Volume = π x r x r x h**, or **V = πr²h**)

EXAMPLE

What is the volume of a barrel that is 36 inches high and has a radius of 8 inches?

$V = \pi r^2 h$ or $V = \pi \times r \times r \times h$
$V = 3.14 \times 8$ in. $\times 8$ in. $\times 36$ in.
$V = 7{,}234.56$ cubic inches

Name_____ Date _____

EXERCISE 10: FIGURING THE VOLUMES OF BARRELS

Listed below are the dimensions for barrels that a cooper contracted to make. Figure the volume of the special-order barrels using the formula from the previous page. Remember, the answers you get will really be approximations. Barrels are not perfect cylinders since they are smaller at either end than at the middle. Also, since they are hand made, the dimensions will not be accurate. Round off your answers to the nearest cubic inch.

	Radius of the Base	Height	Volume
1.	5 in.	22 in.	_____
2.	7 in.	16 in.	_____
3.	6 in.	17 in.	_____
4.	9 in.	19 in.	_____
5.	6.7 in.	20.6 in.	_____
6.	8.2 in.	19.3 in.	_____
7.	7.1 in.	18.5 in.	_____
8.	$6\frac{1}{2}$ in.	$20\frac{1}{4}$ in.	_____
9.	$9\frac{1}{3}$ in.	$15\frac{1}{6}$ in.	_____
10.	$11\frac{1}{5}$ in.	$17\frac{1}{8}$ in.	_____

Name _____ Date _____

Carpenters, Artisans, and Craftsmen

While log cabins and sod homes were the kinds of dwellings the pioneers built and lived in, those living in the city, especially the wealthy, lived in larger, more comfortable homes. In early America most information on architecture and house design came from books from Europe, especially England. Talented home owners with skilled carpenters, craftsmen, and artisans combined their talents to build some very beautiful homes.

In New England, wood was abundant and was used as the main building material. Important men, especially those in southern New England, often chose masonry as the basic material for their homes. Those who chose masonry for their homes needed to decide if they wanted a house made of brick or stone. The decision was often made on the basis of which of the two materials was available locally. If a quarry was nearby, the house most generally was made of stone. If there was no quarry, but a supply of good clay was available, bricks were made and used.

Brick had many advantages over other building materials and was chosen frequently. Bricks were relatively cheap, easy to use, easy to transport, and uniform in size. They also gave an attractive appearance when the house was completed. Brick did not need painting and many of the homes and buildings built of brick in the Colonial and Revolutionary Eras still stand.

Early carpenters and craftsmen built elaborate and intricately designed homes with tools that would be considered crude by today's standards. They were able to build these elegant homes because of their knowledge of mathematics. Here are some of the ways carpenters and craftsmen used mathematics when they built homes.

EXERCISE 11: FIGURING THE BOARD FEET IN LUMBER

Lumber was purchased by the board foot. In order to figure the board feet in lumber, the carpenter multiplied the width of the board (in inches) by the length of the board (in inches) by the thickness of the board (in inches) and then divided the product by 144. **Width″ x Length″ x Thickness″ ÷ 144 = board feet**. The result was the number of board feet in a board.

Example: A board that is 16 feet long by 8 inches wide and is 1 inch thick is how many board feet?

First, multiply 16′ x 12 = 192″ to get the length in inches.
Then, multiply 192″ x 8″ x 1″ = 1,536″ ÷ 144 = 10.67 board feet of lumber.

Figure the board feet in each board below. Round off your anwer to the nearest board foot.

1. 12 ft. x 4 in. x 4 in. = _____

2. 13 ft. x 8 in. x 2 in. = _____

3. 18 ft. x 9 in. x 1 in. = _____

4. 15 ft. x 6.5 in. x 2 in. = _____

5. 22.2 ft. x 16 $\frac{1}{2}$ in. x 1 in. = _____

6. 18 $\frac{1}{4}$ ft. x 6 $\frac{1}{8}$ in. x 4 in. = _____

Name_____ Date _____

EXERCISE 12: FLOOR, WALL, AND CEILING MEASUREMENTS

In order to find the number of square **feet** in a floor or wall, multiply the length by the width or height (in feet). In order to find the number of square **yards** in a floor or wall, multiply the length by the width or height (in feet) and then divide the product by nine. Since there are nine square feet in one square yard, the result will be square yards.

EXAMPLE

How many square yards are in a floor 16 feet wide and 18 feet long?
16′ x 18′ = 288 sq. ft. 288 ÷ 9 = 32 sq. yds. There are 32 square yards in a 16′ x 18′ floor.

How much would it cost a builder if he were to plaster the walls and ceiling of a room 16′ long, 18′ wide, and 11′ high, if the plaster cost 12¢ per square yard?

Step One: Figure the square footage of the ceiling.

16′ x 18′ = 288 square feet.

Step Two: Figure the square footage of the walls. Two of the walls are 16′ wide, and two are 18′ wide. All of the walls are 11′ high.

2(16′ x 11′) + 2(18′ x 11′) = 748 square feet.

Step Three: Add the square footage of the ceiling and the walls together and divide by nine since there are nine square feet for each square yard.

288 + 748 = 1036 ÷ 9 = 115.11 square yards of plaster are needed for the room.

Step Four: Multiply the number of square yards by the cost of the plaster per square yard.

115.11 x 0.12 = $13.81 = Cost to plaster the room.

Figure the cost to plaster the following rooms. Be sure to include the ceiling in your calculations. Carry your answer out to the nearest cent.

1. What will it cost to plaster a room that is 18′ by 22′ and is 10′ high with plaster costing 15¢ per square yard?

_____

2. What will it cost to plaster a room that is 22′ by 20′ and is 12′ high with plaster costing 13¢ per square yard?

_____

Name _____   Date _____

EXERCISE 12: FLOOR, WALL, AND CEILING MEASUREMENTS (CONTINUED)

3. What will it cost to plaster a room that is 24′ by 23′ and is 11′ high with plaster costing 12¢ per square yard?

_____

4. What will it cost to plaster a room that is 19′ by 15′ and is 9′ high with plaster costing $13\frac{1}{2}$¢ per square yard?

_____

5. What will it cost to plaster a room that is 18′ by 22′ and is 10′ high with plaster costing $12\frac{3}{4}$¢ per square yard?

_____

6. What will it cost to plaster a room that is 22′ by 20′ and is 12′ high with plaster costing 14.7¢ per square yard?

_____

7. What will it cost to plaster a room that is 25′ by 23′ and is 11′ high with plaster costing 13.25¢ per square yard?

_____

8. What will it cost to plaster a room that is 19′ by 15′ and is 9′ high with plaster costing $16\frac{1}{8}$¢ per square yard?

_____

9. What will it cost to plaster a room that is 18′ by 24′ and is 10′ high with plaster costing 15.75¢ per square yard?

_____

10. What will it cost to plaster a room that is 19′ by 16′ and is 9′ high with plaster costing $17\frac{1}{2}$¢ per square yard?

_____

Name _____ Date _____

Masonry

The mason worked with stone and bricks. One of his jobs was to figure the number of bricks needed to build a wall. Since bricks were a standard size, 8 inches by 4 inches by 2 inches, builders knew that including mortar, there were 22.5 bricks in a cubic foot.

EXERCISE 13: HOW MANY BRICKS TO BUILD A HOUSE?

In the following problems you are to figure the number of bricks needed to build a home and the cost of those bricks.

EXAMPLE

How many bricks are needed for a wall 10 feet high, 1 foot thick, and 16 feet long?

Step 1: Find the number of cubic feet in the wall by multiplying the dimensions of the wall. This is the same formula used to find the volume of a rectangular solid.

> (v = lwh)
> 10′ x 1′ x 16′ = 160 cubic feet

Step 2: Find the number of bricks needed for the wall by multiplying the number of cubic feet in the wall by the number of bricks in a cubic foot.

> 160 x 22.5 = 3,600 bricks needed

Step 3: Since bricks cost $7.50 per thousand, divide the number of bricks needed by 1,000, and then multiply by $7.50 to find the cost of the bricks.

> 3,600 ÷ 1,000 = 3.6 x $7.50 = $27.00

Complete the following problems. While a mason would not purchase partial bricks, for the sake of this exercise, your final answers should be carried out three places past the decimal point and rounded off to two places. Also, use the full measurements given for each wall. Do not deduct for the thickness of the wall where two walls would meet.

1. How many bricks would be needed for a house whose walls are 20 feet high, 1 foot thick, 16 feet long, and 16 feet wide? Deduct 200 cubic feet for doors and windows after you have figured the total cubic feet for the house. You would not put bricks in the ceiling or floor and you should not consider the bricks needed for the gable. The gable is the triangular section of wall at the end of the pitched roof. It is the space between the two slopes of the roof.

     a. Number of bricks needed. _____

     b. How much would it cost if bricks were $7.50 per thousand? _____

    26

Name_____ Date _____

EXERCISE 13: HOW MANY BRICKS TO BUILD A HOUSE?
(CONTINUED)

2. How many bricks would be needed for a house whose walls are 22 feet high, 18 inches thick, 94 feet long, and 46 feet wide? Deduct 620 cubic feet for doors and windows.

       a. Number of bricks needed. _____

       b. How much would it cost if bricks were $7.48 per thousand? _____

3. How many bricks would be needed for a house whose walls are 18 feet high, 16 inches thick, 62 feet long, and 38 feet wide? Deduct 590 cubic feet for doors and windows.

       a. Number of bricks needed. _____

       b. How much would it cost if bricks were $7.50 per thousand? _____

4. How many bricks would be needed for a house whose walls are 32 feet high, 20 inches thick, 58 feet long, and 32 feet wide? Deduct 610 cubic feet for doors and windows.

       a. Number of bricks needed. _____

       b. How much would it cost if bricks were $7.33 per thousand? _____

5. How many bricks would be needed for a house whose walls are 14 feet high, 12 inches thick, 70 feet long, and 20 feet wide? Deduct 490 cubic feet for doors and windows.

       a. Number of bricks needed. _____

       b. How much would it cost if bricks were $7.40 per thousand? _____

Name_____ Date _____

EXERCISE 14: HOW MANY BRICKS TO BUILD A SIDEWALK

Brick homes in the colonies often had sidewalks made of bricks. In order to figure the number of bricks needed to build a sidewalk, you need to know how many bricks are in a square foot and how many square feet are in the sidewalk.

EXAMPLE

Determine the number of bricks needed and figure the cost of building a sidewalk that is 34 feet by 4 feet. Remember, we are figuring the number of **square** feet in this project, not the number of **cubic** feet. There are 4.5 bricks to the square foot. Assume bricks cost $7.50 per thousand.

Step 1: Find the number of square feet in the sidewalk by multiplying the length by the width. (A = lw)

34′ x 4′ = 136 square feet in the sidewalk.

Step 2: Find the number of bricks needed by multiplying the square footage of the area to be paved by the number of bricks needed to pave a square foot.

136 x 4.5 = 612 bricks needed

Step 3: Since the bricks cost $7.50 per thousand, divide the number of bricks needed by 1,000, and then multiply by $7.50 in order to find the cost of the bricks needed.

612 ÷ 1,000 = 0.612 x $7.50 = $4.59

Find the number of bricks necessary for the following projects. Round your answer off to the nearest whole brick. As you work the problems, it may seem your answers for the cost are too low to be accurate, but remember, this is what the project cost over 200 years ago.

1. How many bricks would be needed and what would the cost be for a sidewalk that is 32 feet long and 20 inches wide?

a. Number of bricks needed. _____

b. How much would it cost if bricks cost $7.47 per thousand? _____

Name _____ Date _____

EXERCISE 14: HOW MANY BRICKS TO BUILD A SIDEWALK (CONTINUED)

2. How many bricks would be needed and what would the cost be for a sidewalk that is 125 feet long and 18 inches wide?

      a. Number of bricks needed. _____

      b. How much would it cost if bricks cost $7.49 per thousand? _____

3. How many bricks would be needed and what would the cost be for a sidewalk that is 275 feet long and 24 inches wide?

      a. Number of bricks needed. _____

      b. How much would it cost if bricks cost $7.49 per thousand? _____

4. How many bricks would be needed and what would the cost be for a sidewalk that is 320 feet long and 36 inches wide?

      a. Number of bricks needed. _____

      b. How much would it cost if bricks cost $7.50 per thousand? _____

5. How many bricks would be needed and what would the cost be for a sidewalk that is 90 feet long and 48 inches wide?

      a. Number of bricks needed. _____

      b. How much would it cost if bricks cost $7.45 per thousand? _____

Name _____ Date _____

Shingles

In the mid 1800s builders devised a formula to figure the number of shingles needed for a roof.

Rule: To find the number of shingles required in a roof, multiply the number of square feet in the roof by 8 if the shingles are exposed 4.5 inches or by 7.5 if exposed 5 inches.

EXERCISE 15: HOW MANY SHINGLES TO COVER A ROOF?

Example: How many shingles will it take to cover a house with a roof that is 42 feet long and measures 20 feet to the peak of the roof (20 feet wide on one side).

Step 1: Multiply the length of the roof by the width.
42' x 20' = 840' square feet
This gives you the area from the edge of the roof to the peak. In other words, it is one-half of the total area of the roof.

Step 2: Multiply the area by two to find the total area for the roof.
840 sq. ft. x 2 = 1,680 sq. ft.

Step 3: If the shingles are to be exposed 4.5 inches, multiply by 8.
1,680 sq. ft. x 8 = 13,440 shingles

Step 4: If the shingles are to be exposed 5 inches, multiply by 7.5.
1,680 sq. ft. x 7.5 = 12,600 shingles

Figure the number of shingles needed for the following roofs. Round off your answers to the nearest whole shingle.

1. A roof 44' x 22' to the peak of the house with shingles exposed 4.5 inches. _____

2. A roof 53' x 20' to the peak of the house with shingles exposed 4.5 inches. _____

3. A roof 38' x 23' to the peak of the house with shingles exposed 5 inches. _____

4. A roof 64.2' x 32.4' to the peak of the house with shingles exposed 5 inches. _____

5. A roof 62.7' x 31.5' to the peak of the house with shingles exposed 5 inches. _____

6. A roof 51.3' x 28.4' to the peak of the house with shingles exposed 5 inches. _____

7. A roof $50\frac{1}{2}$' x $26\frac{3}{4}$' to the peak of the house with shingles exposed 5 inches. _____

8. A roof $39\frac{1}{8}$' x $19\frac{1}{16}$' to the peak of the house with shingles exposed 4.5 inches. _____

9. A roof $41\frac{1}{3}$' x $24\frac{5}{6}$' to the peak of the house with shingles exposed 4.5 inches. _____

10. A roof 46.3' x 23' to the peak of the house with shingles exposed 5 inches. _____

Ferries and Bridges

The first settlers in America did not travel far from the coast. The forest was thick, there were no roads, and the colonists did not have horses or carriages. As the population began to grow and colonists needed to travel between the colonies, they began to use Indian trails. These trails were very narrow and could only be traveled on foot, or on horseback once horses were introduced to the colonies. The trails were gradually widened, and coaches, wagons, carts, and carriages were able to go from colony to colony. Even after the roads were widened to accommodate wagons and carriages, most travelers carried an axe to help them get through the underbrush. Even up until the time of the Revolution, America had few good roads.

Another challenge for travelers was crossing streams and rivers. Ferries and a few bridges were built to allow transportation across rivers and streams. The ferries were private enterprises, and there was a fee to use them. While some bridges were free, others were not.

When a bridge was needed to cross a stream or river, the townspeople would vote if they wanted to fund the project. If they did not, an individual might decide to build the bridge. If he did, then he was able to charge a fee from travelers to recover his expenses.

Ferrying travelers across deep or treacherous rivers was a way to make a lot of money in the early nineteenth century. Travelers were at the mercy of the ferryboat owner. They had to pay what he demanded or try to get across the river on their own. Travelers considered the ferryboat owner nothing more than a robber.

The ferryboat was a long boat big enough for a wagon and six horses. It was propelled by poles, oars, ropes, or even by sail. The sides of the boat were low and both ends were sloped so that passengers could get on and off easily.

Here is what one man charged to ferry people across a river.

RATES FOR FERRY

Each foot passenger: $2\frac{1}{2}$¢

Each live sheep, goat, hog, or calf: $1\frac{1}{2}$¢

Each horned cow, horse, donkey, mule, or ox: 8¢

Each rider and horse or mule: $11\frac{3}{4}$¢

Each two-wheel carriage or cart drawn by one horse, donkey, or mule: $16\frac{1}{4}$¢
   Add 5¢ for each additional horse, donkey, or mule

Each four-wheel pleasure wagon drawn by one horse, donkey, or mule: $23\frac{1}{2}$¢
   Add $10\frac{1}{2}$¢ for each additional horse, donkey, or mule

Each stage coach drawn by one horse, donkey, or mule: $16\frac{1}{4}$¢
   Add $15\frac{1}{4}$¢ for each additional horse, donkey, or mule

Each freight wagon drawn by one horse, donkey, or mule: $14\frac{1}{2}$¢
   Add 5¢ for each additional horse, donkey, or mule

Each sleigh or sled drawn by one horse, donkey, or mule: $13\frac{1}{2}$¢
   Add 5¢ for each additional horse, donkey, or mule

Name _____   Date _____

EXERCISE 16: FIGURING FERRYBOAT INCOME

During one month the ferryboat carried the following people, wagons, and livestock from one side of the river to the other. Figure out how much income the ferryboat owner made. Figure your answer to the nearest whole cent.

1. 125 foot passengers _____

2. 350 live sheep _____

3. 212 live goats _____

4. 119 live hogs _____

5. 75 live calves _____

6. 56 horned cattle _____

7. 16 horses _____

8. 13 mules _____

9. 5 oxen _____

10. 35 riders on horses _____

11. 23 riders on mules _____

12. 19 two-wheel carriages or carts drawn by one horse or mule _____

13. 22 two-wheel carriages or carts drawn by two horses _____

14. 15 two-wheel carriages or carts drawn by two mules _____

15. 33 four-wheel pleasure wagons drawn by one horse or mule _____

16. 13 four-wheel pleasure wagons drawn by two horses or mules _____

17. 12 four-wheel pleasure wagons drawn by four horses or mules _____

18. 28 stage coaches drawn by six horses or mules _____

19. 12 stage coaches drawn by four horses or mules _____

20. 18 freight wagons drawn by two horses or mules _____

21. 14 freight wagons drawn by four horses or mules _____

22. 22 freight wagons drawn by six horses or mules _____

23. 13 freight wagons drawn by eight horses or mules _____

24. 2 sleds each drawn by two mules _____

25. Total Income for Month _____

The General Store

Just about anything farmers and townspeople needed was sold at the general store. There were food items such as molasses, rum, brandy, gin, cider, oysters, salt, tea, coffee, flour, cheeses, crackers, sugar, and dried fish, just to list a few. Although the general store sold clothing, people made most of their own clothes from cloth, ribbon, buttons, and sewing supplies either purchased or ordered at the general store. The general store also stocked household items such as earthenware crocks, lamps, glasses, tableware, bowls, and pitchers. There were cigars, patented medicines, shaving soaps, razors, cough drops, pens, and paper. The general store was a treasure house of necessities.

The general store was the hub of the community. Citizens would assemble at the store to joke and talk about the crops or politics. Since there was no mail delivery to homes in early America, people would come to the store, which often served as the post office, to pick up their mail or to mail a letter. Until the mid 1800s it did not cost anything to send a letter. The postage was paid by the person receiving the letter. The cost of the letter was determined by the distance the letter was sent and the number of pages it contained. A letter containing only one sheet sent over several hundred miles could cost a day's wages.

Illuminated by candles and oil lamps, the general store was a dark and gloomy place due to the lack of windows. Windows were not built into the walls of the general store for two reasons. First, since so many goods were stocked and sold, the store owners built shelves all the way to the ceiling in order to store their goods. Second, it was to the advantage of the store owner to keep the place dark so that customers were unable to see the quality of the goods they were buying. The only windows were in the front of the store, and there were often goods hanging there making the interior quite dim.

Stores opened early in the morning and were often open until late in the evening. The owner could not always operate the store by himself, so he had apprentices to help him. These apprentices were usually members of the owner's family who wanted to learn the trade and were willing to work for board and lodging and little or no pay. The apprentices swept the store, tended to the fire in the stove, and made deliveries.

The prices for goods were negotiable. That meant there was no set price for the items, so the customer and the owner would bargain or haggle over the price. There were times when no money would change hands during a transaction. The owner would sometimes exchange goods for goods, or barter. Women would bring in butter, eggs, or chickens to pay for the things they wanted to purchase. Their husbands might barter with wheat or other farm products. Customers sometimes could not pay for the merchandise at the time they needed the items, so accounts were kept and payments were made, sometimes over a period of many months.

The store owner obviously tried to sell his merchandise for more than he had paid for it. If he was successful, he made a **profit** on the transaction. If he sold the merchandise for less than he had paid for it, then he realized a **loss** on the transaction. The profit or loss is the difference between the cost of an item and the amount for which it is sold.

Name _____ Date _____

EXERCISE 17: PROFIT OR LOSS AT THE GENERAL STORE

Rule: In order to find the profit or loss of an item when the cost and the percentage of profit or loss are given, you multiply the percentage of profit or loss by the cost and round off to the nearest cent. If the transaction is a profit, you add the cost and the amount of profit in order to find the selling price. If the transaction is a loss, you subtract the amount of loss from the cost in order to find the selling price.

EXAMPLES

Flour that cost $7.52 per barrel was sold at 11% profit. What was the amount of profit, and what was the selling price per barrel?

$7.52 x 0.11 = .8272 or 83¢ profit

$7.52 (Cost of the item) + 0.83 (profit) = $8.35 selling price per barrel

Flour that costs $7.52 per barrel was sold at 11% loss. What was the amount of loss, and what was the selling price per barrel?

$7.52 x 0.11 = 0.8272 or 83¢ loss

$7.52 (Cost of the item) – 0.83 (loss) = $6.69 selling price per barrel

Find the amount of profit or loss and the selling price for the following items.

1. Flour costing $7.68 per barrel was sold at 10% profit. What was the amount of profit, and what was the selling price per barrel?

a. Profit _____

b. Selling price _____

2. Flour costing $7.93 per barrel was sold at 9% loss. What was the amount of loss, and what was the selling price per barrel?

a. Loss _____

b. Selling price _____

Name_____ Date _____

EXERCISE 17: PROFIT OR LOSS AT THE GENERAL STORE (CONTINUED)

3. A wagon costing $125 was sold at 6% profit. What was the amount of profit, and what was the selling price ?

      a. Profit _____

      b. Selling price _____

4. A wagon costing $147 was sold at 13% discount. What was the amount of loss, and what was the selling price?

      a. Loss _____

      b. Selling price _____

5. A profit of 8.5% was made on a lot of hogs that cost $525. What was the amount of profit, and what was the selling price?

      a. Profit _____

      b. Selling price _____

6. A loss of 3.2% was realized on a lot of hogs that cost $613. What was the amount of loss, and what was the selling price?

      a. Loss _____

      b. Selling price _____

7. What was the amount of profit and what was the selling price on cloth that cost 37¢ per yard and was sold at a 20% profit?

      a. Profit _____

      b. Selling price _____

8. What was the amount of loss and what was the selling price on cloth that cost 42¢ per yard and was sold at an 8% loss?

      a. Loss _____

      b. Selling price _____

Name_____ Date _____

EXERCISE 18: PERCENTAGE OF PROFIT OR LOSS

Rule: In order to find the percent of profit or loss of an item when the cost and the selling price are given, first find the difference between the cost and selling price. This gives you the actual amount of profit or loss. If the transaction is a profit, divide the amount of profit by the cost in order to find the percentage of profit. If the transaction is a loss, divide the amount of loss by the cost in order to find the percentage of loss. Round your answer off to the nearest whole percent.

EXAMPLES

A merchant purchased wheat at $1.20 per bushel and sold it for $1.45. What percentage of profit was made on the transaction?

$1.45 - $1.20 = 25¢ profit

0.25 ÷ 1.20 = 0.20 or a 20% profit

A merchant purchased wheat at $1.49 per bushel and sold it for $1.32. What percentage of loss was made on the transaction?

$1.49 - $1.32 = 17¢ loss

0.17 ÷ 1.49 = 0.11 or an 11% loss

Find the percentage of profit or loss for the following transactions.

1. A merchant sold cloth at $2.90 per yard that cost $3.10 per yard. What was his percentage of loss?_____

2. A merchant sold cloth at $3.52 per yard that cost $3.00 per yard. What was his percentage of profit?_____

3. A merchant sold coffee at 26¢ per pound that cost 21¢ per pound. What was his percentage of profit? _____

4. A merchant sold coffee at 20¢ per pound that cost 23¢ per pound. What was his percentage of loss? _____

5. A merchant bought a wagon for $310 and sold it for $375. What was his percentage of profit? _____

6. A merchant bought a wagon for $332 and sold it for $305. What was his percentage of loss? _____

7. A merchant bought a general store for $5,000 and sold it for $6,125. What was his percentage of profit? _____

8. A merchant bought a general store for $5,200 and sold it for $4,600 What was his percentage of loss? _____

Name_____ Date _____

EXERCISE 19: VISITING THE GENERAL STORE

A visit to the general store was a happy event that often included the whole family. Essential goods that couldn't be grown, made, or bartered were available at the general store. The store had something for everyone. There were candies, toys, slates for school, and spelling books for the children. Items such as cloth, ribbon, spices, crocks, baskets, and food interested mothers. Fathers bought axes, saws, gunpowder, and lead balls for muskets and rifles. If there was something that a settler needed but that was not at the store, the storekeeper could order it, and the item would be delivered from a large city by boat or wagon.

Purchasing goods was not the only reason to go to the general store. The general store was often the post office, and it was a place for settlers to gather and visit with each other. Since neighbors lived so far from one another and working on farms took so much time, settlers might go months without seeing their friends or neighbors.

The general store was not like the modern supermarket. Since money was scarce, storekeepers would keep accounts, and customers would purchase items on credit. When the customers sold a crop or made some money some other way, it was time to come in and settle the bills. Some customers did not pay in money but in goods. A farmer, for example, might bring the shopkeeper several dozen eggs or some cured bacon. The shopkeeper put a value on these items and would credit the farmer's account by this amount. The shopkeeper, of course, would then try to sell these items for more than he paid the farmer.

Here is the transaction of a typical family. The McIntosh family made the following purchases:

12 lbs. and 3 oz. of butter at $9\frac{1}{2}$ cents per pound. (There are 16 ounces in a pound.)
3 sacks of coffee weighing $3\frac{1}{2}$ pounds per sack at $12\frac{1}{2}$ cents per pound.
4.25 dozen eggs at $8\frac{1}{2}$ cents per dozen.
125 pounds of sugar at $6\frac{1}{4}$ cents per pound.
$12\frac{3}{4}$ yards of cloth at 75 cents per yard.

The father brought the storekeeper 35 bushels of wheat and 6 bushels of potatoes. The storekeeper agreed to accept the wheat and potatoes as payment on the McIntosh account and credited Mr. McIntosh $1.37 per bushel for the wheat and $1.01 per bushel for the potatoes.

Name _____ Date _____

EXERCISE 19: VISITING THE GENERAL STORE (CONTINUED)

    The McIntosh account is shown below. Fill in the purchases and payments and find the current balance for the McIntosh account. The balance shown on May 29 is the amount John McIntosh owed to the store owner on that date. Whenever a purchase is made, the amount should be entered into the debit column and added to the balance. The new balance should then be entered in the balance column. Whenever a payment is made, the amount is posted to the Credit column, and the amount is subtracted from the balance. The new balance should then be entered in the balance column.

John McIntosh				
Date	**Entry**	**Debit**	**Credit**	**Balance**
May 29	Balance			$37.15
June 10	12 lbs. and 3 oz. of butter at $9\frac{1}{2}$ cts. per lb.			
"	3 sacks of coffee weighing $3\frac{1}{2}$ lbs. per sack at $12\frac{1}{2}$ cts. per lb.			
"	4.25 doz. eggs at $8\frac{1}{2}$ cts. per doz.			
"	125 lbs. sugar at $6\frac{1}{4}$ cts. per lb.			
"	$12\frac{3}{4}$ yds. of cloth at 75 cts. per yd.			
"	Traded 6 bu. potatoes at $1.01 per bu.			
"	Traded 35 bu. wheat at $1.37 per bu.			
"	Balance			

Name _____ Date _____

Peddlers

Storekeepers did not like peddlers, but the settlers did. The idea of the peddler developed out of necessity. Since the roads were bad, traveling was slow, and the population was sparse and scattered throughout the country, most families made traveling to the general store an all-day affair. In addition, the trip to town was a social event, so the family felt a need to dress up in order to make a good appearance. A trip to the general store was an enjoyable activity, but when peddlers came directly to the home, valuable time and energy was saved. Of course, there was not the selection that the general store offered, but peddlers did provide many essential items pioneers needed so that families were able to postpone their trips to the store.

Like the owner of the general store, the peddler also bartered his goods for goods the pioneers might have. The peddler might swap cloth or razors for pork and eggs. He might trade pots and pans for pelts and then sell the pelts to a fur trader in town.

EXERCISE 20: FIGURING A PEDDLER'S INVENTORY

Here is a list of the inventory of a typical peddler. Calculate the total value for each item as well as the total value of the inventory. Round your answers to the nearest cent. One gross is equal to 12 dozen, and a fathom is equal to 6 feet.

1. 25 duck trousers at $0.70 each _____
2. $6\frac{1}{2}$ dozen pocket looking glasses at 36 cents per dozen _____
3. 12 packs horse bells at $5.00 per pack _____
4. 1 pound of thread at 75 cents per pound _____
5. 15 pounds vermilion at $85\frac{1}{3}$ cents per pound _____
6. 7 dozen small bone combs at 15 cents each _____
7. 11 feet gold chain at $62\frac{1}{2}$ cents an inch _____
8. 8 dozen gilt buttons at $8\frac{1}{2}$ cents each _____
9. $2\frac{1}{2}$ dozen 9-inch butcher knives at $1.68 each _____
10. $2\frac{1}{2}$ dozen 8-inch butcher knives at $1.25 each _____
11. 8 Indian knives at $1.25 each _____
12. 1 gross fancy rings at $1.32 each _____
13. 1.2 dozen dirk knives at $2.62\frac{1}{2}$ each _____
14. 6 packs playing cards at 15 cents a pack _____
15. 21 fathoms large blue beads at $5\frac{1}{2}$ cents a foot _____
16. $4\frac{1}{2}$ fathoms large red beads at $5\frac{1}{2}$ cents a foot _____
17. 9 dressing combs at 50 cents each _____

Name_____ Date _____

EXERCISE 20: FIGURING A PEDDLER'S INVENTORY (CONTINUED)

18. 18 fathoms large green beads at $5\frac{1}{2}$ cents a foot _____

19. $37\frac{1}{2}$ bunches second-sized blue beads at 3 cents a bunch _____

20. 5 pair Mack blankets at $4.25 pair _____

21. 23 small tin pans at $8\frac{1}{4}$ cents _____

22. 173 pounds lead at $6\frac{1}{4}$ cents pound _____

23. 1 bag 60 pounds coffee at 15 cents per pound _____

24. 1 bag 60 pounds sugar at 12 cents per pound _____

25. 2 bags 63 pounds gunpowder at 30 cents per pound _____

26. 71 pounds tobacco at $12\frac{1}{2}$ cents per pound _____

27. 3 silver pencil cases at $1.00 each _____

28. 78 pounds shot at 25 cents per pound _____

29. 15 axes at $2.52 each _____

30. 17 beaver traps at $9.00 each _____

31. 34 pounds flour at 10 cents per pound _____

32. 12 pounds allspice at 56 cents per pound _____

33. 215 pounds raisins at 22 cents per pound _____

34. 23 finger rings at $5.03 per gross _____

35. 17 assorted bridles at $7.50 each _____

36. 5 pairs spurs at $2 per pair _____

37. 19 pounds horse shoes and nails at $2.07 per pound _____

38. 23 handkerchiefs assorted at 2 cents each _____

39. 18 looking glasses at $0.50 each _____

40. 2 gross flints at $0.59 per dozen _____

41. $56\frac{1}{4}$ yards French calico at $0.35 per yard _____

42. $54\frac{1}{6}$ yards blue calico at $0.28 _____

43. 31 yards green calico at $0.20 per yard _____

44. $81\frac{1}{3}$ yards brown calico at $0.21 per yard _____

45. 65 yards gray calico at $0.225 yard _____

46. $1\frac{1}{4}$ dozen bandanas at $0.36 per dozen _____

47. 18 iron buckles assorted at $0.12 each _____

48. $12\frac{1}{5}$ pounds dried fruit at $0.25 cents per pound _____

49. 19 pounds of washing soap at $0.32 cents per pound _____

50. 22 pounds shaving soap at $0.35 per pound _____

51. $17\frac{1}{3}$ pounds large brass wire at $2.01 per pound _____

52. 1 dozen French lace shawls at $2.50 each _____

53. Total _____

Mathematics in Business

In the Revolutionary Era, businessmen did not have computers, calculators, or even adding machines to do the many calculations that were necessary in order to transact their business. Calculations were done by hand. However, businessmen learned that they made certain calculations every day, every week, or every month, so many of them decided to record these calculations on a chart. When they needed to use them, they simply used the chart rather than calculating each time. One calculation that businessmen needed to do often was to figure the amount of wages to be paid to workers. The calculation would take time because a businessman might have many workers and craftsmen being paid different wage rates. In addition to different rates, some may have been hired only for a day while others might be hired for a week or a month. To speed up his bookkeeping, a businessman might create a **wages table** similar to the one below.

EXERCISE 21: COMPLETING A WAGES TABLE

Complete the wages table on the next page. The **weekly** rates are given in bold print at the top of the columns. You are to figure the hourly rate and the daily rate for each weekly wage rate and then fill in the chart so a business owner could look at it to see how much to pay someone who had worked four hours or one day and six hours.

EXAMPLES

At this particular company, the workers worked 10 hours each day for six days a week. This was not typical for most workers of this period. Most worked more.

If a worker was paid $3 per week, how much did he earn per hour?

10 hours per day x 6 days per week = 60 hours per week.

The weekly rate is divided by the number of hours per week in order to find the hourly wage.

$3.00 \div 60 = 0.05$ The worker who earns $3.00 per week earns $0.05 per hour.

If a worker was paid $3 per week, how much did the worker earn per day?

10 hours per day x $0.05 per hour = $0.50 per day.
Or, $3 per week ÷ 6 days per week = $0.50 per day.

Name _____ Date _____

EXERCISE 21: COMPLETING A WAGES TABLE (CONTINUED)

Complete the wages table below. Round each answer off to the nearest cent, but use the original number found for the hourly and daily rates to figure the rest of the rates in each column.

Example: $3.50 ÷ 60 = 0.0583 = 0.06 for one hour   0.0583 x 3 = 0.17 for three hours

0.0583 x 10 = 0.583 = 0.58 for one day   0.583 x 3 = 1.749 = 1.75 for three days

Wages Table for Days and Hours at Given Rates Per Week

Weekly Rate		$3.00	$3.50	$4.00	$4.50	$5.00	$5.50	$6.00	$6.50	$7.00	$7.50	$8.00	$9.00	$10.00
Hourly Rate / Hours Worked	1	$0.05												
	2	$0.10												
	3													
	4													
	5													
	6													
	7													
	8													
	9													
Daily Rate / Days Worked	1													
	2													
	3													
	4													
	5													

Name _____ Date _____

EXERCISE 22: CONVERSION OF COMMON FRACTIONS TO DECIMAL FRACTIONS

Another calculation that businessmen in the Revolutionary Period needed to complete often was the conversion of common fractions to decimal fractions. Money and goods were so scarce that fractions played an important role in this era. Eggs might cost $8\frac{1}{4}$ cents a dozen. A worker might be paid $13\frac{1}{2}$ cents an hour. Since decimal fractions are easier to work with than common fractions and money is based on the decimal system, businessmen needed to be able to convert between the two. Rather than figure out this conversion each time it was needed, businessmen often created a chart to save them time. One such table is shown below. However, the decimal equivalents are not shown.

In order to change a common fraction to a decimal fraction, divide the numerator by the denominator. Example: What is the decimal equivalent of $\frac{1}{2}$?

$$1 \div 2 = 0.5 \quad \text{Therefore } \tfrac{1}{2} = 0.5$$

Fill in the missing decimal equivalents in the following table.

Table Showing the Equivalent Decimals of Common Fractions

Common Fraction	$\frac{1}{2}$	$\frac{1}{3}$	$\frac{2}{3}$	$\frac{1}{4}$	$\frac{3}{4}$	$\frac{1}{5}$	$\frac{2}{5}$	$\frac{3}{5}$	$\frac{4}{5}$
Decimal Equivalent	0.5								
Common Fraction	$\frac{1}{6}$	$\frac{5}{6}$	$\frac{1}{8}$	$\frac{3}{8}$	$\frac{5}{8}$	$\frac{7}{8}$	$\frac{1}{12}$	$\frac{5}{12}$	$\frac{7}{12}$
Decimal Equivalent									
Common Fraction	$\frac{11}{12}$	$\frac{1}{16}$	$\frac{3}{16}$	$\frac{5}{16}$	$\frac{7}{16}$	$\frac{9}{16}$	$\frac{11}{16}$	$\frac{13}{16}$	$\frac{15}{16}$
Decimal Equivalent									

Slavery in the Colonies

Slaves arrived in America at Jamestown, Virginia, in 1619. There were few slaves at first, but with the development of the plantation system in the southern colonies, the number of slaves imported for agricultural labor greatly increased. Plantations relied heavily on human effort to work the tobacco, sugar, cotton, rice, and indigo fields. While slaves were primarily used in agriculture in the southern and mid-Atlantic colonies, in the northern colonies, slaves were used as servants.

As the colonies grew, northern colonists used fewer and fewer slaves, until, for the most part, they disapproved of slave labor. However, the southern colonies' economy gradually became dependent on slavery. Plantation owners purchased African slaves to work their plantations. By the latter part of the eighteenth century, slave labor was vital to the southern economy, and the demand for African workers caused a steady increase of their population.

The slavery issue continued to split the nation further during the mid nineteenth century, as the North and South refused to agree on the issue. Events such as the Kansas-Nebraska Act, the *Dred Scott* Decision, the publication of *Uncle Tom's Cabin*, and the Harpers Ferry insurrection all helped lead the country to the Civil War.

During the Civil War, thousands of slaves left the plantations and cities of the South and sought refuge in the North. Following the victory over the Confederacy by the Union forces, the Thirteenth Amendment to the Constitution was passed, freeing the slaves.

Here is a list of the number of slaves counted in the 1790 census.

State	Number of Slaves	State	Number of Slaves
CONNECTICUT	2,648	NEW YORK	21,193
MAINE	0	PENNSYLVANIA	3,707
MASSACHUSETTS	0	VIRGINIA	292,627
NEW HAMPSHIRE	157	GEORGIA	29,264
RHODE ISLAND	958	NORTH CAROLINA	100,783
VERMONT	0	SOUTH CAROLINA	107,094
DELAWARE	8,887	MARYLAND	103,036
NEW JERSEY	11,423		

EXERCISE 23: SLAVERY BAR GRAPH

The above information can be displayed as a graph. A bar graph of the number of slaves in 1790 would provide a visual comparison of the number of slaves in each state. Make a bar graph of the above information using the form on the next page.

Name _____ Date _____

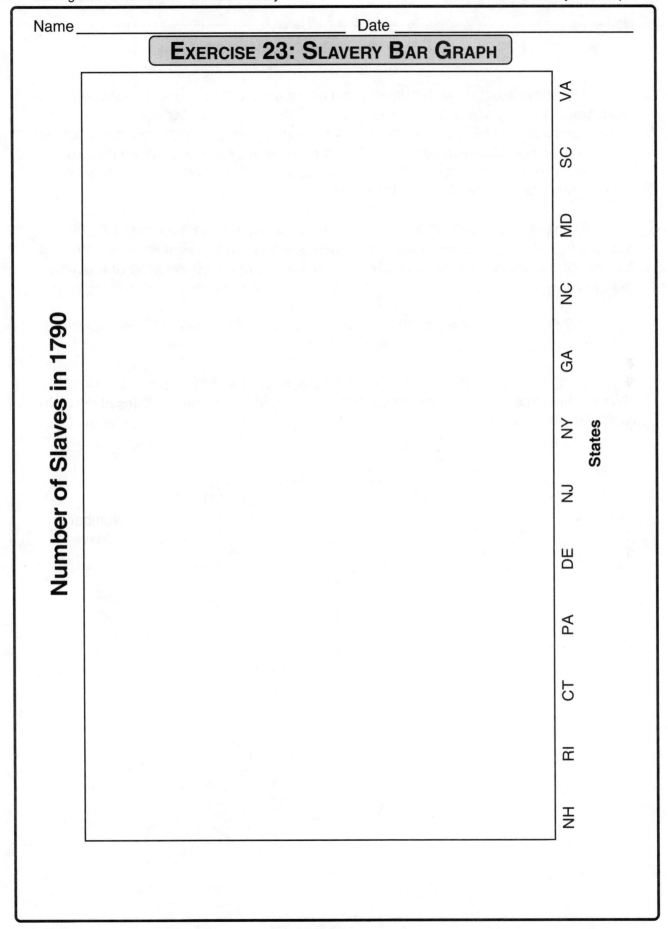

Number of Slaves in 1790

NH   RI   CT   PA   DE   NJ   NY   GA   NC   MD   SC   VA

States

Name _____ Date _____

EXERCISE 24: SLAVERY CIRCLE GRAPH

The same information displayed in the bar graph on page 45 can be displayed in a circle graph. When you make a circle graph, the circle represents 100% of the information you are displaying. In this case, the entire circle would represent the total number of slaves in the colonies in 1790, which was 681,777. Each state would represent a percentage of that total. One could find the percentage each state represents by dividing each state's total by the total number of slaves for all of the states.

Example: The total number of slaves in all of the states in 1790 was 681,777. Virginia had 292,627 slaves. In order to find the percentage of slaves in Virginia, divide the total number of slaves in Virginia (292,627) by the total number of slaves in the colonies (681,777).

292,627 ÷ 681,777 = 0.4292 Virginia had 42.92 % of the slaves in the states listed in 1790.

Using the information on the preceding page, complete the following circle graph showing the percentage of slaves for each of the states in 1790. Shade each section of the circle a different color.

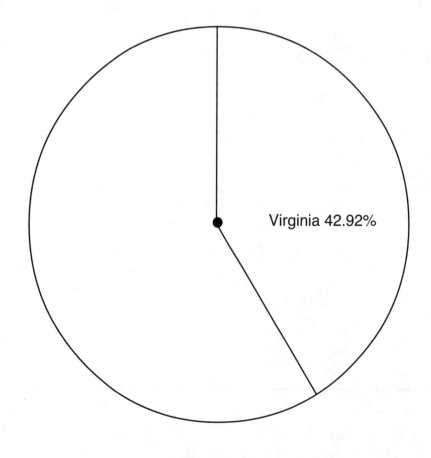

Virginia 42.92%

EXERCISE 25: USING RATIOS TO COMPARE SLAVES TO FREEDMEN

The 1860 census revealed the total number of slaves, as well as the total number of people of African descent who were free for a number of states. Slaves who had been freed were called freedmen.

There are several ways to compare these numbers. Frequently, **ratios** are used to compare two numbers. A ratio is sometimes called a **ratio comparison**.

Here is an example. Suppose there are four hundred students in your school and you discover there are 2,000 books in the school library. How could you best compare the number of students in school with the number of books in the school library? One way to compare them is by division. When you compare two numbers by division, you are finding the **ratio** of these numbers. Ratios are fractions. They can be proper fractions such as 400/2,000. Or they may be improper fractions such as 2,000/400.

It can easily be seen that if you were to reduce the proper fraction in the example above, you would get $\frac{1}{5}$. This ratio can be expressed in one of the following ways:

- 1 to 5 (In words)
- 1:5 (Colon notation)
- $\frac{1}{5}$ (Fraction notation)

What we are basically saying is the ratio of students to books is 1:5. In other words, there is one student for every five books in the school.

This same information may also be used to express the ratio comparing the number of books to students. In other words it can be expressed as:

- 5 to 1
- 5:1
- $\frac{5}{1}$

When we express the ratio in this way, we are comparing the number of books to students. We are saying there are five books for every student in school.

Name _____ Date _____

EXERCISE 25: USING RATIOS TO COMPARE SLAVES TO FREEDMEN (CONTINUED)

In this exercise you are to find the ratio of slaves to freedmen in 1860 in the states listed and then figure the decimal equivalent. If necessary, carry your answer to four places past the decimal point and round off to three places. The ratio of slaves to freedmen in Kansas in 1860 is given as an example.

Number of African Slaves in Kansas in 1860: 2
Number of free blacks in Kansas in 1860: 625

Ratio: 2:625
To find the decimal equivalent divide: 2 ÷ 625 = 0.0032 = 0.003

There were 0.003 slaves in Kansas for every free black in 1860.

Round off your answers to three places past the decimal point if necessary.

1860

State	Number of Slaves	Free Black Population	Ratio of Slaves to Freedmen	Decimal Equivalent
1. DELAWARE	1,798	19,829	_____	_____
2. KANSAS	2	625	2:625	0.003
3. VIRGINIA	490,865	58,042	_____	_____
4. ALABAMA	435,080	2,690	_____	_____
5. ARKANSAS	111,115	144	_____	_____
6. FLORIDA	61,745	932	_____	_____
7. GEORGIA	462,198	3,500	_____	_____
8. LOUISIANA	331,726	18,647	_____	_____
9. MISSISSIPPI	436,631	773	_____	_____
10. NORTH CAROLINA	331,059	30,463	_____	_____
11. SOUTH CAROLINA	402,406	9,914	_____	_____
12. TEXAS	182,566	355	_____	_____
13. KENTUCKY	225,483	10,684	_____	_____
14. MARYLAND	87,189	83,942	_____	_____
15. TENNESSEE	275,719	7,300	_____	_____

The Rise of Agriculture in America

When the colonists came to America, most relied on the land for their food. Since there were no machines and few horses, mules, oxen, or other animals to help with the plowing and hauling, most of the farms were very small. Many were as small as fifty acres. Few were larger than 200 acres. However, between the years of 1840 and 1860, tremendous changes in agriculture took place. Horses, mules, and oxen became commonplace, and agriculture in America passed from the era of hand tools to the era of animal power.

Implements changed as well. Once, only simple hand tools were used. New hand tools were invented that enabled one man to cut four to six acres of standing grain in one day. By the middle of the nineteenth century, more improvements, including the McCormick Reaper, permitted a man to work larger farms. In the South, slavery enabled landowners to have very large plantations that produced tobacco and cotton for export.

All of these changes contributed to the growth of farms. Not only did the number of farms increase, but the size of the farms increased as well. In 1860, the census reported the following numbers and sizes of farms in the following states.

FARMS IN 1860

| | Farm Acreage | | | | | | |
	3–9	10–19	20–49	50–99	100–499	500–999	+1,000
CONNECTICUT	936	2,081	6,898	8,477	6,666	39	4
MAINE	1,719	5,435	23,838	19,611	5,061	9	2
MASSACHUSETTS	2,032	4,196	11,765	10,831	6,703	29	0
NEW HAMPSHIRE	859	1,855	7,584	11,338	8,759	45	4
RHODE ISLAND	261	552	1,740	1,747	1,053	11	0
VERMONT	321	1,158	6,187	11,702	1,505	92	1
DELAWARE	63	215	1,226	2,208	2,862	14	0
NEW JERSEY	1,059	2,390	7,138	9,652	7,198	17	6
NEW YORK	5,232	12,310	54,502	73,037	50,132	225	21
PENNSYLVANIA	4,821	12,343	45,234	57,624	35,923	61	15
VIRGINIA	2,351	5,565	19,584	21,145	34,300	2,882	641
NORTH CAROLINA	2,050	4,879	20,882	18,496	19,220	1,184	311
SOUTH CAROLINA	352	1,219	6,695	6,980	11,369	1,359	482

Name_____ Date _____

EXERCISE 26: USING RATIOS TO COMPARE FARM SIZES

Use the chart on the previous page to answer the following questions.

1. Which state had the most 3- to 9-acre farms? _____

2. Which state had the least 3- to 9-acre farms? _____

3. Which state had the most 10- to 19-acre farms?_____

4. Which state had the least 10- to 19-acre farms?_____

5. Which state had the most 20- to 49-acre farms? _____

6. Which state had the least 20- to 49-acre farms?_____

7. Which state had the most 50- to 99-acre farms? _____

8. Which state had the least 50- to 99-acre farms?_____

9. Which state had the most 100- to 499-acre farms? _____

10. Which state had the least 100- to 499-acre farms? _____

11. Which state had the most 500- to 999-acre farms? _____

12. Which state had the least 500- to 999-acre farms? _____

13. Which state had the most farms of 1,000 acres or more? _____

14. Which state had the second to the most farms of 1,000 acres or more? _____

Write the ratio of farms of 3 to 9 acres to the number of farms 500 to 999 acres and then figure the decimal equivalent. Connecticut is given as an example:

Number of farms of 3 to 9 acres: 936
Number of farms 500 to 999 acres: 39

936:39   936 ÷ 39 = 24

There are 24 3- to 9-acre farms for every one 500- to 999-acre farm.

Figure your answer to three places past the decimal and round off to two places if necessary.

15. What is the ratio of farms of 3 to 9 acres to farms 500 to 999 acres for Connecticut?

_____

16. What is the ratio of farms of 3 to 9 acres to farms 500 to 999 acres for Maine?

_____

Name _____ Date _____

EXERCISE 26: USING RATIOS TO COMPARE FARM SIZES
(CONTINUED)

17. What is the ratio of farms of 3 to 9 acres to farms 500 to 999 acres for Massachusetts?

_____

18. What is the ratio of farms of 3 to 9 acres to farms 500 to 999 acres for New Hampshire?

_____

19. What is the ratio of farms of 3 to 9 acres to farms 500 to 999 acres for Rhode Island?

_____

20. What is the ratio of farms of 3 to 9 acres to farms 500 to 999 acres for Vermont?

_____

21. What is the ratio of farms of 3 to 9 acres to farms 500 to 999 acres for Delaware?

_____

22. What is the ratio of farms of 3 to 9 acres to farms 500 to 999 acres for New Jersey?

_____

23. What is the ratio of farms of 3 to 9 acres to farms 500 to 999 acres for New York?

_____

24. What is the ratio of farms of 3 to 9 acres to farms 500 to 999 acres for Pennsylvania?

_____

25. What is the ratio of farms of 3 to 9 acres to farms 500 to 999 acres for Virginia?

_____

26. What is the ratio of farms of 3 to 9 acres to farms 500 to 999 acres for North Carolina?

_____

27. What is the ratio of farms of 3 to 9 acres to farms 500 to 999 acres for South Carolina?

_____

28. What is the ratio of total farms of 3 to 9 acres to total farms of 500 to 999 acres?

_____

Important Civil War Locations

When a person wants to show a location on a map, it is sometimes convenient to make a **coordinate graph**. A coordinate graph consisting of a **horizontal** line, known as the X axis, and a **vertical** line, known as the Y axis, can be used to indicate a specific location. Each axis is divided into coordinates numbered from the center, which is called the **origin**. The numbers at the left and the bottom of the origin are numbered -1, -2, -3, and so on. The numbers at the right and the top of the origin are numbered +1, +2, +3, and so on. These numbers are called **coordinates**.

In order to find a point on a coordinate graph, one must find the coordinate on the horizontal axis that indicates where the point is located in relation to the origin. Then one must find the coordinate on the vertical axis that indicates where the point is located in relation to the origin. By following the lines of these two points to the place they meet, any point on the coordinate graph may be found.

Look at the coordinate graph on page 53, which shows some of the locations that were important in the Civil War. Find the point labeled "Washington." If you look across the horizontal axis you will find the X coordinate is +3. If you look up the Y axis you will find the Y coordinate is also +3. This pair of numbers, +3 and +3, are called an **ordered pair** and are put in parentheses with a comma between them. When writing an ordered pair, put the X coordinate, which describes how far the point is to the left or to the right of the origin first. The Y coordinate, which describes how far the location is above or below the origin, should be listed second. (+3, +3)

In the following exercise you will locate various sites important to the Civil War in the coordinating graph shown . **The locations on the graph are not drawn to scale, and not all of the locations important in the Civil War are shown.**

Name _____ Date _____

EXERCISE 27: READING A COORDINATE GRAPH

List the coordinates for the following locations.

Example: Washington (+3, +3)

1. Atlanta _____

2. Appomattox _____

3. Chattanooga _____

4. Charleston _____

5. Cincinnati_____

6. Columbia _____

7. Columbus _____

8. Gettysburg_____

9. Milledgeville _____

10. Norfolk _____

11. Perryville _____

12. Philadelphia _____

13. Raleigh_____

14. Savannah _____

15. Wilmington _____

Name _____ Date _____

Agriculture in the United States Since 1860

In the 1860s most people lived on farms. Many of the farms were self-sufficient, which meant that the farmers raised food for their own use. The products produced on the farm were not usually sold for money. Instead, most of the products produced on the farm were used by the farmer's family. Any surplus products were often exchanged for other products that the farmer needed.

After the 1860s, significant changes were taking place in farming. Americans began to think about moving west of the Mississippi River to the Great Plains. On the Great Plains there were many acres of fertile farm land that were ready to be settled. The Civil War was over, and many soldiers looked to settle the Great Plains and begin a new life. Immigrants were coming to the United States, and many of them also saw the Great Plains as a wonderful opportunity.

EXERCISE 28: SURVEYING THE LAND OF THE FRONTIER

When people began to settle the Great Plains, they had their land surveyed. Surveys were necessary to identify where specific pieces of property were located, and they provided the farmer with a description of his property. The survey system used was a **rectangular system.** The basic unit of the rectangular system was the **township.** The township was a square that measured six miles on each side. Each township was divided into 36 smaller squares called **sections.**

1. The following square has been divided into 36 smaller squares. Some of the sections have been numbered. Number the remaining sections by writing the correct number on each unnumbered section.

1			4		6
		9			
13			16		
	20				
			28		
		33			

Answer the following:

2. Townships are divided into (a)_____ smaller squares called (b) _____ . The townships measure six miles on each side, so each township covers (c) _____ square miles. Each section is (d)_____ mile(s) on each side and covers (e)_____ square mile(s).

    54

Name _____ Date _____

EXERCISE 28: SURVEYING THE LAND OF THE FRONTIER (CONT.)

Let's assume that the township discussed below represents a township surveyed in one of the states west of the Mississippi River. Townships are named, so this township will be named North Creek.

With the rectangular system, each of the 36 sections of land in a township contains 640 acres of land. Each of the sections is then divided into one-fourths called **quarter sections**. Each of the quarter sections contains 160 acres. The quarter sections can be further divided into fourths of 40 acres each.

At the right is Section 16 of North Creek Township divided into quarter sections. Section 16 above has been divided into four equal parts. You will also note the letters N, S, E, and W indicating compass directions north, south, east, and west.

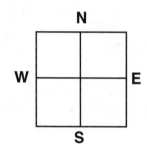

Refer to the diagram of Section 16, and answer the following questions.

3. Section 16 contains _____ acres.

4. Each of the one-fourth parts (quarter sections) of Section 16 contains _____ acres.

5. Why do you think each of the small squares in Section 16 is called a "quarter section"?

_____

_____

Let's learn how the quarter sections are referred to in Section 16. There are four quarter sections in any section. The quarter sections are labeled as part of the section in which they are located. The quarter sections for Section 16 are labeled as the Northwest Quarter of Section 16 (NW $\frac{1}{4}$), the Southwest Quarter of Section 16 (SW $\frac{1}{4}$), the Northeast Quarter of Section 16 (NE $\frac{1}{4}$), and the Southeast Quarter of Section 16 (SE $\frac{1}{4}$).

6. The diagram below is Section 16 of North Creek Township. Each of the quarter sections has a letter on it. Place one of the letters on the blank next to the description below that identifies that quarter section.

a) _____ SE $\frac{1}{4}$ b) _____ SW $\frac{1}{4}$

c) _____ NE $\frac{1}{4}$ d) _____ NW $\frac{1}{4}$

7. Color in the Northwest Quarter of Section 16.

Name_____ Date _____

EXERCISE 28: SURVEYING THE LAND OF THE FRONTIER (CONT.)

Now let's take the Northwest Quarter Section of Section 16 ("A" in the diagram on the previous page) and divide it into four equal parts.

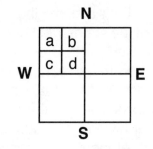

The diagram at right represents the Northwest Quarter Section of Section 16 divided into four equal parts.

8. The Northwest Quarter Section has _____ acres.

9. Each of the small squares in the Northwest Quarter Section has _____ acres.

The small square labeled "a" in the diagram of the Northwest Quarter Section is identified as the Northwest Fourth of the Northwest Quarter Section of Section 16 in North Creek Township.

10. The small square labeled "b" is identified as the _____ Fourth of the _____ _____ Section of _____ 16 in _____ _____ Township.

11. The small square labeled "c" is identified as the _____ _____ of the _____ _____ _____ of_____ 16 in _____ _____ Township.

12. The small square labeled "d" is identified as the _____ _____ of the _____ _____ _____ of_____ 16 in _____ _____ Township.

Name _____ Date _____

EXERCISE 28: SURVEYING THE LAND OF THE FRONTIER (CONT.)

For the next exercise, refer to the diagram of Section 16 below. When an individual buys property, the specific location of the property is based on the township, section, and part of the section where the property is located. Let's look at how a piece of property, which is located in Section 16, North Creek Township, in the State of Nebraska, might be described.

The year is 1866 and Sam and Lana Jones have just been married in Ohio. Sam is 21 years old and a veteran of the Civil War. The Homestead Land Act gives Sam the opportunity to buy 160 acres of land in the Great Plains area for $1.25 per acre. Sam and Lana decide that they will move to the Nebraska Territory and become farmers. They move to the Nebraska Territory and pay for the 160 acres. They are then given a deed to the property with the following description.

"All that part of the Southeast Quarter of Section Sixteen (16) North Creek Township, situated in Calhoun County, Nebraska Territory."

13. Draw a small square to locate Sam and Lana's 160 acres on the map below.

North Creek Township

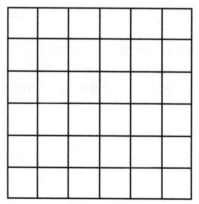

In the year 1873, farm prices are very low. Sam and Lana owe money and decide they will sell part of their property to pay bills. They decide to sell the property described below.

"All that part of the Southeast Fourth of the Southeast Quarter Section of Section Sixteen (16) North Creek Township, situated in Calhoun County, Nebraska Territory."

14. Draw a small square to locate the property that Sam and Lana are going to sell.

15. How many acres of land are they going to sell? _____

16. They will own _____ acres after selling the above described property.

Name _____ Date _____

EXERCISE 29: COMPARING FARMING AND NONFARMING POPULATIONS

Farming in the United States after 1860 underwent many changes. One of the major changes had to do with the percent of the total U. S. population that lives on farms. Complete the following questions to find how the farm population has changed since 1860.

1. In 1860, 7,000,000 people lived in the United States. Sixty-five percent of the people were living on farms. In 1860 there were _____ people living on farms.

2. In 1890, 70,000,000 people lived in the United States. Forty-two percent of the people were living on farms. In 1890 there were _____ people living on farms.

3. In 1930, 120,000,000 people lived in the United States. Twenty-five percent of the people were living on farms. In 1930 there were _____ people living on farms.

4. In 1960, 190,000,000 people lived in the United States. Twenty percent of the people were living on farms. In 1960 there were _____ people living on farms.

5. In 1990, 250,000,000 people lived in the United States. Three percent of the people were living on farms. In 1990 there were _____ people living on farms.

6. On the line graph below, plot the points for the percent of the population living on farms for the years 1860, 1890, 1930, 1960, and 1990. Place a dot on the graph to locate the percent of the population you think will be living on farms in the year 2010.

```
70%
60%
50%
40%
30%
20%
10%
 5%
 3%
 2%
      1860      1890      1930      1960      1990      2010
```

7. In your own words explain what the above graph tells you.

_____

_____

_____

_____

Name _____ Date _____

EXERCISE 30: PIE GRAPHS AND POPULATION

A pie graph is a circle that can be used to show information visually. A pie graph can be used to visually compare the number of people living on farms with those not living on farms for specific years. Below are two circles. One circle represents the percent of farmers compared to the total population in 1860. The other circle compares the percent of farmers to the total population in 2000.

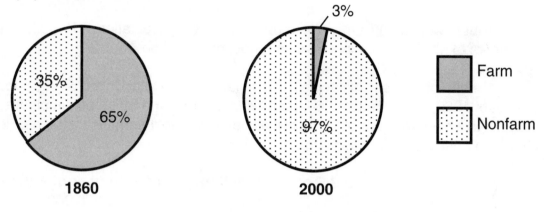

1860   **2000**

Refer to the above circle graphs and answer the following questions.

1. What percent of the population lived on farms in 1860? _____ %

2. What percent of the population lived on farms in 2000? _____ %

In 1860 the population of the United States was 7,000,000. In 2000 the population of the United States was 276,000,000.

3. How many million people lived on farms in 1860? _____

4. This figure is represented by the (shaded, dotted) area on the circle for 1860. (Circle one.)

5. How many million people lived on farms in 2000? _____

6. This figure is represented by the (shaded/dotted) area on the circle for 1990.

Name _____ Date _____

EXERCISE 31: RATIOS AND POPULATION

In understanding the role of the farmer, it is important to look at the ratio between people living on farms and those not living on farms for different periods from 1860 to 1990. A ratio can be expressed as a fraction. In the exercise that follows, you will learn to use ratios to compare the number of farmers to nonfarmers.

EXAMPLE

If there were 5,000 farmers in a county with a total population of 15,000, then the ratio of farmers to nonfarmers expressed as a fraction would be $\frac{5000}{15000}$ or $\frac{1}{3}$.

Determine the ratio of people living on farms to the total United States population for the years 1860, 1890, 1930, 1960, and 1990. Express the ratios as simple fractions. All figures have been rounded off to make it easier for you to determine the ratios. Refer to the chart and answer the questions below.

Year	U.S. Total Population	Total Number of Farmers
1860	7,000,000	5,000,000
1890	70,000,000	45,000,000
1930	120,000,000	30,000,000
1960	200,000,000	40,000,000
1990	240,000,000	6,000,000

1. The ratio of farmers to total population in 1860 was _____ .

2. The ratio of farmers to total population in 1890 was _____ .

3. The ratio of farmers to total population in 1930 was _____ .

4. The ratio of farmers to total population in 1960 was _____ .

5. The ratio of farmers to total population in 1990 was _____ .

Answer the following using population figures for the United States.

6. In 1860 five million people were producing food for _____ million people.

7. In 1890 forty-five million people were producing food for _____ million people.

8. In 1930 thirty million people were producing food for _____ million people.

9. In 1960 forty million people were producing food for _____ million people.

10. In 1990 six million people were producing food for _____ million people.

11. Since 1960, the farm population has been (decreasing/increasing) while the total population has been (decreasing/increasing).

Name_____ Date _____

Understanding Supply and Demand
EXERCISE 32: THE LAW OF SUPPLY

Farmers, like other businessmen, have found that the amount of money they make is related to the **laws of supply and demand**. The **law of supply** states that as prices go up, producers are willing to produce more. When prices go down, producers will produce less. The graph below is a supply graph that shows what happens to the supply of bushels of wheat as the price per bushel increases. Supply curves are often used to show the number of products a farmer or business is willing to produce at different prices.

Example: If the price of wheat is $0.50 per bushel then a farmer is willing to produce 10 bushels—indicated by the letter "A" on the supply curve where $0.50 meets 10 bushels.

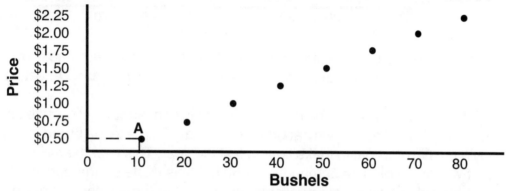

Refer to the above supply curve and answer the following questions.

1. The farmer is willing to produce _____ bushels at $0.75 per bushel.

2. The farmer is willing to produce _____ bushels at $1.25 per bushel.

3. The farmer is willing to produce _____ bushels at $2.00 per bushel.

Problem: You are a farmer living in Kansas on a wheat farm. To raise a bushel of wheat, you have to buy things like seed, fertilizer, and machinery.

Answer the following questions.

4. It costs you $1.00 to raise a bushel of wheat. The price you can get for a bushel of wheat is $0.75. On the blanks below tell what you would do and why.

_____

_____

5. It costs you $1.00 to raise a bushel of wheat. The price you can get for a bushel of wheat is $2.00. You have a farm on which you can produce 5,000 bushels of wheat. On the blanks below tell what you would do and why.

_____

_____

Name _____ Date _____

EXERCISE 33: THE LAW OF DEMAND

The **law of demand** states that as prices go up, people demand less. As prices go down, people demand more. **Demand** is the ability and willingness of consumers to buy something.

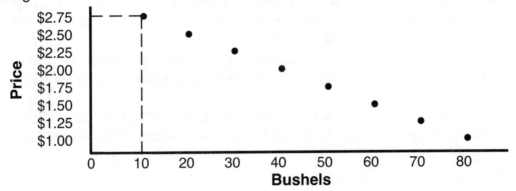

To read the demand curve, it is important to note that as the number of bushels increases, the price decreases. Let's look at an example of how demand affects price.

Example: There are 50 families living in a town. There is one farmer just outside town who raises wheat. The 50 families in town eat bread every day. To make the bread, each family needs to buy a bushel of wheat to make flour to last the year. This year the farmer has only 10 bushels of wheat to sell. The demand is for 50 bushels. Note on the demand line that when only 10 bushels of wheat are available, the price the farmer can get per bushel is $2.75—the point where the vertical line from 10 bushels meets the horizontal line from $2.75.

Refer to the above demand curve and answer the following questions.

1. The demand curve shows that when twenty bushels of wheat are available, the farmer will receive $ _____ per bushel.

2. The demand curve shows that when fifty bushels of wheat are available, the farmer will receive $ _____ per bushel.

3. The demand curve shows that when seventy bushels of wheat are available, the farmer will receive $ _____ per bushel.

4. When the supply of bushels of wheat increases, the price of wheat (increases/ decreases).

5. When the supply of bushels of wheat increases, the _____ for wheat decreases.

6. When the supply of bushels of wheat decreases, the price of wheat (increases/ decreases).

7. When the supply of bushels of wheat decreases, the _____ for wheat increases.

Name _____ Date _____

EXERCISE 34: SUPPLY AND DEMAND FOR WHEAT

Problem: The year is 1870, and you have moved to the Great Plains to farm in the area that will, in the future, become the state of Nebraska. You are raising wheat. There is a great demand for wheat, and the price per bushel is $1.50. It costs you $1.00 to produce a bushel of wheat.

   Answer the following questions.

1. You are making a profit of $ _____ on each bushel of wheat.

2. You find that you can produce an extra 1,000 bushels of wheat next year. This will make you an extra income of $ _____ .

3. Next year I (will/will not) produce the extra 1,000 bushels because _____

_____

_____

Problem: The year is 1880, and you have been farming for ten years. When you first started farming, you were producing one thousand bushels of wheat per year. By using improved farming methods, you have been able to increase production and can now produce 5,000 bushels per year. Wheat prices per bushel have been $1.50 per bushel, and it has been costing you $1.00 per bushel to produce the wheat, so your income has increased each year.

4. In the ten years you have increased your production of wheat by _____ bushels.

5. In the ten years you have increased your income by $ _____ per year.

Problem: A new invention, the reaper, has just become available. The reaper will make it possible for you to harvest much more grain in the same amount of time that you have needed to harvest the 5,000 bushels. You think that with the new reaper you could easily harvest an additional 2,000 bushels per year. The reaper costs $1,000.00, which you can borrow at the bank and repay over a two-year period in two equal payments. You will have to pay an interest rate of six percent per year on the unpaid balance.

6. At the end of the first year, you will owe the bank one-half of the $1,000.00 which is $ _____ .

7. At the end of the first year, you will owe the bank an additional $ _____ for interest on the one thousand dollars that you have borrowed for the year.

8. At the end of the first year, you will owe a total of $500.00 plus $ _____ interest, for a total of $ _____ .

9. At the end of the second year, you will owe the bank $500.00 plus the interest for that $500.00, which is a total of $ _____ .

Name _____ Date _____

EXERCISE 34: SUPPLY AND DEMAND FOR WHEAT (CONTINUED)

Problem: In deciding to buy the reaper, you find that you can produce an extra 2,000 bushels with the reaper. You have determined in the questions above how much the reaper will cost. You know that wheat has been selling for $1.50 per bushel and the cost of producing a bushel has been $1.00.

10. If you buy the reaper you will have $ _____ after making the payment to the bank.

11. I (will/will not) buy the reaper because _____

_____

_____

_____

Problem: You buy the reaper and make arrangements with the bank to borrow the money. The next year, the price paid to you for a bushel of wheat is $0.90, but the cost of producing a bushel of wheat is still $1.00.

12. In the space below, explain the problem the change in price of wheat from $1.50 to $0.90 presents for you as a farmer.

_____

_____

_____

_____

_____

_____

13. In the space below, explain how you will address the problem presented in Question 12.

_____

_____

_____

_____

_____

_____

Name _____ Date _____

EXERCISE 35: INFLATION AND CORN PRODUCTION

One of the major problems faced by farmers during the period from 1860 to the present has been the fact that in many years the farmer's cost of production is higher than the price received for the product. One reason the cost of producing a product keeps increasing is **inflation**. Inflation is the amount by which a given product increases in price over a given time. Inflation is usually expressed as a percent.

Problem: You are a young farmer raising corn in the Midwest. The first year you farm, the cost of producing a bushel of corn is $2.50. You are receiving $3.50 per bushel. However, in years three, four, and five, the supply of bushels of corn increases significantly. The demand for corn falls, so the price per bushel decreases. However, your cost of production for fertilizer, seed, and fuel has been increasing. This increase is called inflation.

Refer to the chart below and solve the problems that follow.

	Cost to produce bushel of corn	Price received for bushel of corn
Year 1	$2.50	$3.50
Year 2	$2.55	$3.40
Year 3	$2.75	$3.00
Year 4	$2.86	$3.00
Year 5	$3.00	$2.90
Year 6	$3.06	$4.00
Year 7	$3.15	$4.10

1. The cost to produce a bushel of corn increased by $ _____ from Year 1 to Year 2.

2. This increase in cost to produce a bushel of corn is   a) 2   b) 4   c) 10   d) 6   percent.

3. The cost to produce a bushel of corn increased by $ _____ from Year 3 to Year 4.

4. The increase in cost to produce a bushel of corn from Year 3 to Year 4 is   a) 4   b) 2   c) 10   d) 6   percent.

5. The inflation rate in percent from Year 4 to Year 5 is _____ percent.

6. The demand for corn (increased/decreased) in Years 6 and 7.

7. You make the decision to (increase/decrease) corn production for Year 8.

8. In the space below explain your thinking in arriving at the decision you made in #7.

_____

_____

_____

_____

_____

Name _____ Date _____

EXERCISE 36: HELPFUL FARMING INVENTIONS

Throughout the years, farmers have continued to become more productive. New types of farming methods and improved seeds, plants, and animals were important. The move from horse power to machines brought major changes in the lives of farmers.

Each of the paragraphs below describes one of the following terms. The terms include the names of people, machines, plants, or farming methods. Read each paragraph and write the term described on the blank beside the paragraph. Refer to history books or other resources to help you determine the correct answers.

reaper	truck	plow	tractor	combine
Burbank	contour farming		crop rotation	dry farming
Carleton	Whitney			

_____ 1. This man made major improvements in the varieties of vegetables, flowers, and fruits that could be grown. Although he developed many new plants, he became famous for the development of a new variety of potato.

_____ 2. This method of farming helped keep the soil from blowing away. Farmers plowed furrows that followed the curves of the hills rather than plowing a straight line.

_____ 3. This man became famous for developing a new variety of wheat. The variety he developed would grow and produce in very dry regions. Many of the drier lands of the Great Plains became more productive with this new variety of wheat.

_____ 4. Using this improved method, farmers found that by alternating crops grown on a plot of land the yield of the alternated crops could be improved. Farmers might alternate from year to year the growing of corn, wheat, and beans on the same plot.

_____ 5. This invention took the place of horses for pulling farm machinery. It was a gas-powered machine that farmers rode on while pulling implements over the farm. This invention freed up many acres of land that had been used to produce food for horses.

_____ 6. This invention by Cyrus McCormick was important in decreasing the time and work involved in harvesting a crop.

Name _____ Date _____

EXERCISE 36: HELPFUL FARMING INVENTIONS (CONTINUED)

_____ 7. This machine made it possible for farmers to transport farm products over long distances. It is gas-powered and is very important today in moving farm products across the nation. The machine was made in factories using assembly line production methods developed by Henry Ford. Many of these machines use the super highways for rapid transportation.

_____ 8. This man invented the cotton gin. He also developed the use of interchangeable parts for firearms. Interchangeable parts made possible the development of mass production techniques.

_____ 9. This farming method allowed farmers to conserve moisture for raising crops. Using this method in dry lands, farmers would plant crops on a plot of land every other year. The plot of land was plowed and allowed to collect moisture while no crops were growing on it.

_____ 10. Using this invention, farmers turned the soil. The first improvement of the primitive wooden device involved putting an iron tip on the wooden share. Many farmers refused to use the new invention, fearing that because it was made of iron it would ruin the soil.

Transportation Systems Develop

In the period between 1866 and 1900, there were many changes in the United States. Many people were moving west, industries and factories were developing rapidly and becoming larger requiring many workers, and farmers were producing large crops to be sold. It was a period of boom and bust for those who worked in the factories as well as farmers.

The period between 1866 and 1900 was a time of boundless energy and great optimism. It was also a time of strife, loss of fortunes, and hardship as the nation was testing the limits of a capitalistic economy. Workers sometimes found jobs plentiful, but there were also times of great hardship when factories closed and the unskilled worker suffered most. Farmers found that in many years there was a ready market for their crops. In other years, however, the farmer did not receive enough money to pay for the cost of production.

New inventions were changing the way people worked and lived. Industry and agriculture were developing rapidly. The United States was a large nation and getting larger.

Developing a transportation system that would meet the needs of a rapidly developing nation was important.

EXERCISE 37: WATER TRANSPORTATION

The large system of rivers and lakes has been very important in the development of the United States. When settlers began to move over the Appalachian Mountains, the large rivers and lakes became the major travel routes.

By the 1860s many rivers and lakes in the eastern United States were connected by canals and short rail lines. Men like Andrew Carnegie realized that the natural transportation routes provided by rivers and lakes were important to the developing coal, oil, and iron/steel industries. The growth of these early industries was based on river and lake transportation that would lead to the development of major cities around the Great Lakes.

On a copy of the map of the United States on page 82 locate the following:

Lake Huron	Lake Ontario	Lake Michigan
Lake Erie	Lake Superior	Hudson River
Ohio River	Mohawk River	St. Mary River
St. Lawrence River	Mississippi River	Missouri River
Erie Canal	Buffalo	Syracuse
New York	Baltimore	Philadelphia
St. Louis	New Orleans	

Name _____ Date _____

EXERCISE 38: RAILROAD TRANSPORTATION

From the beginning of the nation to the present, the growth of the United States has depended on a good system of transportation. Rivers and lakes provided a natural transportation system in many parts of the nation; however, the changes in industry and farming after 1860 required a transportation system that extended to the regions of the United States where rivers and lakes were not found. Railroads were the answer. Railroad transportation would become very important following the Civil War.

1. In 1860 there were 5,000 miles of canals in the United States. In the same year, there were 30,000 miles of railroads. The miles of canals were a) $\frac{3}{4}$ b) $\frac{1}{6}$ c) $\frac{2}{3}$ d) $\frac{1}{2}$ of the miles of railroads.

2. In 1860 there were   a) 3   b) 10   c) 2   d) 6   times more miles of railroads than of canals.

Transportation up until the Civil War was mostly by water, horses or oxen, or very short rail lines. Most of the railroads served local regions in the East and South. These railroad lines were very short—often less than 100 miles long. Following the Civil War, however, railroads became very important.

Large numbers of people were moving west. Some were ranchers, some were grain farmers, and some were people seeking gold and silver. There were few large lakes or rivers in the West, so water transportation was not available to most settlements. Transportation by animal was too slow and could not adequately transport the large numbers of people and products that needed to be moved across the United States.

Soon men saw that building railroads in the West offered opportunities that could make them rich. Men like Cornelius Vanderbilt became known as "Railroad Barons." These men became very powerful in the railroad business.

The opening of the West brought new opportunities for the railroads, and soon efforts were underway to build railroads west to California. Thousands of miles of rail were laid between 1870 and 1900. In 1870 there were 50,000 miles of railroad track in the United States. In 1900 there were almost 200,000 miles of track. By 1960 there were 215,000 miles or track, and by 1990 the railroad mileage in the United States was down to 160,000.

Solve the following:

3. The miles of railroad track in 1870 were   a) _____ (fraction) or   b) _____ % of the miles of track in 1900.

4. The miles of railroad track in 1900 were   a) _____ times or   b) _____ % of the miles of track in 1870.

5. The miles of railroad track in 1960 were   a) _____ times or   b) _____ % of the miles of track in 1900.

6. The miles of railroad track in 1990 were   a) _____ (fraction) or   b) _____ % of the miles of track in 1960.

69

Name _____ Date _____

EXERCISE 39: RAILROAD TRANSPORTATION MAP ACTIVITY

Three major railroads were soon connecting the eastern part of the nation with the west. They were the Northern Pacific, the Union/Central Pacific, and the Atlantic Pacific. In addition, the Southern Pacific railroad ran along the Pacific Coast.

Complete the following activity:

Using the symbols (++++++++), draw the Northern Pacific, Union Pacific, Atlantic Pacific, and the Southern Pacific railroads on a copy of the map of the United States on page 82.

- The Northern Pacific railroad began in Duluth and St. Paul, Minnesota; crossed southern North Dakota; went through Miles City, Montana, to Virginia City, Montana; ran across northern Idaho; and then continued west to the coast at Seattle and Tacoma, Washington.

- The Union Pacific began at Council Bluffs, Iowa; went through Ogalla, Nebraska; and continued west to Promontory Point, Utah, where it became the Central Pacific and then went west to Sacramento and San Francisco, California.

- The Atlantic Pacific began at Kansas City, Missouri; continued to Dodge City, Kansas; then went southwest across northern New Mexico and northern Arizona to Los Angeles, California.

- The Southern Pacific railroad ran from Seattle, Washington; through Tacoma, Washington; south to San Francisco and Los Angeles, California.

Answer the following:

1. The Northern Pacific railroad passed through what present-day states?

_____

_____

2. The Union and Central Pacific railroads passed through what present-day states?

_____

_____

3. The Atlantic Pacific railroad passed through what present-day states?

_____

_____

4. The Southern Pacific railroad passed through what present-day states?

_____

Name_____ Date _____

EXERCISE 40: U.S. HIGHWAY SYSTEM MAP ACTIVITY

After 1900 the transportation provided by railroads was not sufficient. As the automobile became an important means of transportation, an extensive system of highways was required.

The network of super highways that now connect all parts of the United States are vital to both the industrial and agricultural development of the nation. When President Dwight D. Eisenhower came to office in 1953, he saw the development of the nation's highways as one of his main objectives.

For the next exercise you will need a map of the United States that shows the major highways and cities.

Locate the following cities by placing a dot for each on a copy of the United States map on page 82.

New York, New York	Cleveland, Ohio	Davenport, Iowa
Des Moines, Iowa	Omaha, Nebraska	Cheyenne, Wyoming
Salt Lake City, Utah	Reno, Nevada	Sacramento, California
San Francisco, California		

Draw a line connecting each of the dots, starting in the East and continuing west. Write the number 80 at various points on the line. This line represents Highway 80, which connects the eastern and western seaboards of the nation.

Refer to a map showing the major highways in the United States and answer the following questions.

1. List some of the larger cities connected by Highway 70. _____

_____

2. List some of the larger cities connected by Highway 20. _____

_____

3. What highway connects Billings, Montana; Casper, Wyoming; Pueblo, Colorado; and El Paso, Texas? _____

4. What major highways run through Denver, Colorado? _____

5. What highway would you travel to go from Chicago, Illinois, through Minneapolis, Minnesota; Fargo, North Dakota; Billings, Montana; Spokane, Washington; and end at Seattle, Washington? _____

6. What highway connects Seattle, Washington; Portland, Oregon; and Los Angeles, California? _____

Name _____ Date _____

EXERCISE 41: COMPARING MODES OF TRANSPORTATION

The following problems are all distance, rate, and time problems. You can find one of these items if you know the other two. You may find that you can use the following formulas.

D = Distance　　　　R = Rate　　　　T = Time
$D = R*T$　　　　　$R = D/T$　　　　$T = D/R$

When President George Washington took office in 1789, he traveled on horseback from Mt. Vernon in Virginia to New York City to be inaugurated. The trip of 240 miles took 12 days.

1. If President Washington traveled for 10 hours each day, it took him _____ hours to travel from Mt. Vernon to New York City.

2. Today, driving a car at a speed of 60 miles per hour, you could travel from Mt. Vernon to New York City in _____ hours.

3. If you choose to fly in a commuter airplane at a speed of 200 miles per hour, you could travel from Mt. Vernon to New York City in _____ hours.

The distance from Washington, D.C., to San Francisco is approximately 2,800 miles. Solve the following problems.

4. A trailer truck transporting fresh produce from San Francisco to Washington, D.C., is traveling at a speed of 60 miles per hour. How many hours will it take the trailer truck to reach Washington, D.C.? _____

Complete the following blanks using the words below.

automobile　　　**rivers**　　　**highway**　　　**railroads**　　　**lakes**

5. Until 1860, (a) _____ and (b) _____ were important methods of transporting people and products. From 1860 to 1900, many (c) _____ were built to improve the nation's transportation system. Since 1900, the invention of the (d)_____ led to the development of the present-day (e) _____ system.

6. On the blanks below, write what you think the next important transportation development will be. _____

_____

Industrial Development

The period from 1865 to 1870 saw the development of large industries. These industries were often controlled by men who used the large size of their companies to run competitors out of business. By 1900 a few of these large companies controlled a large amount of the business. A few men controlled these large businesses. Once the company had forced most of the competitors out, they could raise prices and make large fortunes.

EXERCISE 42: THE IRON/STEEL INDUSTRY DEVELOPS

In the 1850s a very important discovery was made that contributed to the industrialization of America. Henry Bessemer discovered how to burn the impurities out of melted iron. Bessemer discovered that when air was injected into the melted iron, the impurities were burned off as sparks. The burning off of the impurities converted the iron to much stronger and longer-lasting steel. This discovery became very important as the railroad system was rapidly developing and steel rails would last much longer than iron rails. Steel making has remained a major industry in the United States to the present time.

The discovery of a large iron ore deposit in Minnesota resulted in a significant growth of iron- and steel-producing cities in the Great Lakes region. The iron ore mine, named the Mesabi Range, is located at the western tip of Lake Superior. In addition, a large coal field was located near Pittsburgh, Pennsylvania. This was important since coal is necessary to smelt the iron ore to create steel.

Ships loaded with iron ore from the Mesabi Range crossed the Great Lakes, and ships loaded with coal from the Pittsburgh area went upriver to the growing cities of the Great Lakes region. Soon cities like Gary, Indiana; Toledo and Cleveland, Ohio; and Pittsburgh became major iron and steel centers.

Refer to a copy of the United States map on page 82, and locate the following:

1. Place dots to locate the cities Chicago, Cincinnati, Toledo, St. Louis, New Orleans, Gary, Duluth, and Pittsburgh.

2. Draw in the Mississippi River, Ohio River, Hudson River, Wabash River, Illinois River, and the Allegheny River. Locate each of the Great Lakes.

3. Locate the Mesabi Range (iron) using the symbols (Fe Fe Fe).

4. Place the symbol (###) for coal deposits in the area just below Pittsburgh.

Name_____ Date _____

EXERCISE 42: THE IRON/STEEL INDUSTRY DEVELOPS (CONTINUED)

5. On the blanks below, tell how the location of the Mesabi iron ore mine, the coal mines near Pittsburgh, and water transportation influenced the development of iron and steel industries in cities like Pittsburgh, Cleveland, Toledo, and Gary.

_____

_____

_____

_____

_____

_____

_____

_____

   In 1870 the United States was producing 2,000,000 tons of iron/steel. By 1900 production had increased to 10,000,000 tons.

6. The production of iron/steel in 1900 was   a) two   b) three   c) five   d) ten   times the production of 1870.

7. The production of iron/steel in 1950 was 100,000,000 tons. This was   a) ten   b) twenty c) one hundred   d) two   times the production of 1900.

8. The production of iron/steel in 1950 was   a) ten   b) fifty   c) one hundred   d) twenty times the production of 1870.

Industrialization and Labor Unions

Because industries began using mass production techniques, a system called **division of labor** was developed. Workers each performed a specific step and then passed the unfinished product to the next worker. Workers did not have to be highly skilled to complete these jobs. This is what is meant by **unskilled labor**.

The development of large industries like iron and steel, oil, meat processing, and assembly line production of such things as automobiles and farm machinery made it possible for large numbers of unskilled workers to find work. Many of these unskilled workers were people leaving farms or immigrants from foreign lands.

Working conditions were often poor. Many had to work long hours in conditions that were not safe. In some cases the salaries earned were not enough to provide adequately for a man and his family. When the company could not sell its products, the workers were out of work.

Soon the workers were clamoring for better working conditions, but the owners of the factories were reluctant to change. It was also difficult to get elected officials to make laws that would improve their working conditions, since unskilled workers had little political influence.

Finally in May 1886, workers went on strike against the McCormick Harvester Machine Company in Haymarket Square in Chicago, Illinois. Workers wanted an eight-hour work day and improved working conditions. As a result of the conflict between the striking workers and private policemen hired by the McCormick Company, a worker was killed. Later, seven Chicago policemen and four demonstrators were killed.

In addition to strikes, workers also began to organize in labor unions, which tried to negotiate with factory owners to get their working conditions improved. A new labor organization named the American Federation of Labor was formed in 1886 by Samuel Gompers. He believed that improving working conditions, increasing wages, and decreasing hours worked were the important issues that had to be addressed. By the early 1900s, the union was gaining strength and making inroads in improving working conditions.

Name_____ Date _____

EXERCISE 43: THE GROWTH OF LABOR UNIONS

The number of workers available to work in the various jobs in the nation is known as the **labor force**. Not every member of the labor force belongs to a union. The following chart shows the number of workers that were union members for the years 1900, 1920, 1940, 1960, and 1980.

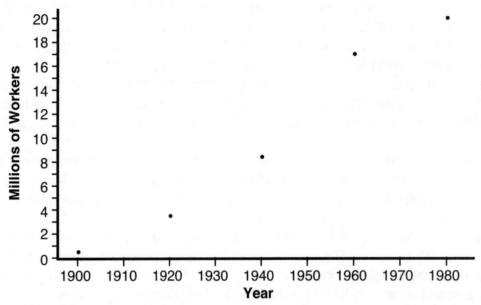

Refer to the graph above and answer the following questions. Read each dot as locating a point that represents either even millions (1,000,000; 2,000,000; and so forth) or even millions plus 500,000.

1. In 1900, _____ workers were union members.

2. In 1920, _____ workers were union members.

3. In 1940, _____ workers were union members.

4. In 1960, _____ workers were union members.

5. In 1980, _____ workers were union members.

6. How many more workers belonged to unions in 1960 than in 1900? _____

7. How many more workers belonged to unions in 1960 than in 1920? _____

8. During which 20-year period did the greatest increase in union membership occur?

_____

Name _____   Date _____

EXERCISE 44: BOOM AND BUST IN THE AMERICAN ECONOMY

When factories were in full production, almost all workers could find jobs. The factories found that there was a market for what they were producing so they began producing more. Soon, however, the factories were producing more than could be sold. The managers of the factories then decided to stop production until the items in stock were sold. When this happened, the factories often stopped hiring workers and laid off many others. This period of full employment followed by a period of high unemployment has been referred to as **"boom and bust"** in the American economy.

In the United States there have been periods when large numbers of people could not find jobs. When this happens, people spend their money only on food and clothing items that are necessary. Sometimes these periods of high unemployment go on for a long time. These are particularly bad times for unskilled workers. When large numbers of people are unemployed and cannot find work the time is referred to as a **depression**.

Major depressions have occurred a number of times since 1860. Three very serious depressions were in 1873, 1893, and 1930. These were periods of "bust" for the workers. Each of these depressions followed times when factories had been running at full capacity. When the factories were running at full capacity, workers had jobs and there was extra money to spend on things besides food and clothing. These were the "boom" periods.

After researching the Great Depression, read the statements below and place a plus sign (+) in the blanks before those statements that you think led to the Great Depression of the 1930s. Discuss your answers with your teacher and other class members.

_____ 1. People were speculating that the price of stocks would continue to rise indefinitely.

_____ 2. More goods were produced during the 1920s than people were willing or able to buy.

_____ 3. People were buying many items on credit.

_____ 4. When the stock market crashed, many companies went broke and people lost their jobs. Without jobs, people stopped buying many of the items that companies were producing.

_____ 5. The government did not have any programs to help people who were out of work.

_____ 6. The government did not have any controls over the stock market and the investments that were made.

Name_____ Date _____

EXERCISE 45: LEARNING ABOUT THE 1920s AND 1930s MATCHING ACTIVITY

The decades of the 1920s and 1930s were times of great change in the United States. The terms below are related to events, inventions, people, and so on that were significant in the 1920s and 1930s. Following the list of terms are statements that can be associated with each of the terms. Identify the statement that defines or explains each term. Write the letter of the statement on the line next to the term the statement identifies. You will need to refer to history books, the Internet, and other sources to verify that you are identifying the correct statement for each term.

_____ 1. Louis Armstrong

_____ 2. Assembly line

_____ 3. Babe Ruth

_____ 4. Black Thursday

_____ 5. Bull market

_____ 6. Al Capone

_____ 7. Jack Dempsey

_____ 8. Depression

_____ 9. Eighteenth Amendment

_____ 10. F. Scott Fitzgerald

_____ 11. Henry Ford

_____ 12. Ernest Hemingway

_____ 13. Herbert Hoover

_____ 14. Hoovervilles

_____ 15. Installment plan

_____ 16. Jazz

_____ 17. KDKA (radio station)

_____ 18. Charles Lindbergh

_____ 19. Model T Ford

_____ 20. Motion picture

_____ 21. New Deal

_____ 22. New York Stock Exchange

_____ 23. Nineteenth Amendment to the

      Constitution

_____ 24. Panic of 1929

_____ 25. Public Works Administration

_____ 26. Radio

_____ 27. Red Grange

_____ 28. Franklin Roosevelt

_____ 29. Speculators

_____ 30. Stockholder

_____ 31. Stocks

_____ 32. George Westinghouse

Name _____ Date _____

EXERCISE 45: MATCHING ACTIVITY (CONTINUED)

A. In August 1920, this amendment was ratified giving women the right to vote.

B. This man made the automobile popular in the United States. He produced the automobiles on an assembly line and sold the Model T at an affordable price.

C. This man invented air brakes for trains in 1869. The air brake made trains safer since the engineer could apply brakes on all of the railroad cars at the same time.

D. This vehicle was developed by Henry Ford. By 1929 over fifteen million of these vehicles had been built using assembly line production.

E. This man was a sports idol of the 1920s and 1930s. He was a great baseball player who hit sixty home runs in one season. One of his most famous exploits occurred in the World Series of 1932 when with two strikes on him he gestured to the point in the stands where he planned to hit a home run.

F. This was a method used by factories for large-scale production. Each person stood and assembled a particular part of a product as it moved along the line before the workers. Henry Ford made it famous in the production of the Model T Ford.

G. This invention was wireless and was installed in many homes in the 1920s. Until television became popular in the 1950s, this was the center of attention in almost every home as people listened to news and entertainment programs.

H. This was a form of music that became popular in the 1920s and 1930s. This music was created by African-American musicians in New Orleans in the late 1800s. Louis Armstrong was the most famous musician playing this music.

I. This method of purchasing items began in the 1920s and 1930s. People could buy things and pay for them using a planned schedule of payments. Typically, the payment included the principal plus an interest amount.

J. He was a great prize fighter and world champion known as the "Manassas Mauler."

K. The first radio broadcast was heard on this station in November 1920. The station was located in Pittsburgh, Pennsylvania.

L. This man wrote *The Great Gatsby*.

M. This man wrote *Farewell to Arms, For Whom the Bell Tolls, The Sun Also Rises,* and *The Old Man and the Sea*. He received the Nobel prize for literature.

N. A famous football player who wore the number 72. He attended the University of Illinois and was known for great runs. He was nicknamed the "Ice Man."

O. This is a time of great unemployment. People are out of jobs and have a very difficult time. Factories and companies are often closed. Although major ones occurred in 1873 and 1893, the last great one in the United States began in 1929 and continued well into the 1930s.

P. This president of the United States was elected in 1928. He believed in a *laissez faire* policy, which meant that the government should not interfere in business. Shortly after he took office, the Great Depression of 1929 began.

Name_____ Date _____

EXERCISE 45: MATCHING ACTIVITY (CONTINUED)

Q. Elected president in 1932, this man instituted the New Deal that brought major changes to the social and economic systems in the United States. Social Security was one of the social programs that began with the New Deal.

R. Rudolph Valentino and Greta Garbo became famous in the 1920s because many cities in the United States had theaters where these could be seen. The greatest star of the 1920s was Charlie Chaplin. The conversations appeared on the screen in writing since sound could not be produced.

S. This was established as a place where stock in companies could be bought, sold, and traded.

T. When a corporation is formed, shares of these are sold on the stock market. A certificate is issued showing the number of shares that are owned. These are often labeled as "common" or "preferred."

U. Time when the stock market crashed in 1929. Many people were soon out of work and some were homeless. Fortunes were lost as the price of stocks plummeted.

V. Communities of homeless who were out of work during the depression that began in 1929. Herbert Hoover was president and thus the name.

W. The social and economic program proposed by President Franklin Roosevelt.

X. Those who invest in the stock market and gamble that stocks will increase or decrease in value.

Y. One of the owners of stock in a corporation.

Z. Name given to a time when most of the stocks on the stock market are going up in price. Indicates that most people are optimistic that good times will come.

AA. Famous criminal of the 1920s.

BB. The amendment that began the era of prohibition—a time when the production or sale of alcoholic beverages was unlawful. This amendment was ratified in 1919 but was repealed by the Twenty-first Amendment in 1933.

CC. Famous jazz musician who got his start in New Orleans. Known affectionately as "Satchmo."

DD. A government program established as part of the New Deal to provide employment for those out of work. The workers were given jobs that involved public works improvements such as buildings, bridges, roads, and parks.

EE. October 24, 1929, the day a great wave of selling occurred on the stock market. The result was fear and panic and the beginning of the Great Depression.

FF. In 1927, he flew *The Spirit of St. Louis* from New York City to Paris, France. He was the first person to fly nonstop across the Atlantic Ocean.

Name _____   Date _____

EXERCISE 46: ENTERTAINMENT AND HEROES OF THE 1920s AND 1930s

In the 1920s and 1930s, various forms of entertainment became important to people. Sports such as boxing, baseball, and football were particularly popular. Basketball, invented by James Naismith in 1891–92, had not yet reached the popularity that it has today. Radio programs and movies also entertained people across the nation. In addition to sports and movie stars, many people followed the exploits of adventurers such as Charles Lindbergh and Amelia Earhart.

Solve the following problems.

1. Babe Ruth hit 60 home runs in 1927. If he came to bat 300 times, he hit a home run every
   a) 1   b) 5   c) 10   d) 4   times at bat.

2. In 1924, the University of Illinois played the University of Michigan in football. Illinois' Red Grange made touchdown runs of 95, 67, 55, 55, and 10 yards. The total yards run for touchdowns was a) _____ . The average yards per touchdown run was b) _____ yards.

3. In 1924, two million homes in the United States had radios. In 1934, twenty million homes had radios. The homes with radios in 1924 was a) 1/10   b) 7/10   c) 3/10   d) 4/10 of the homes with radios in 1934.

4. If admission to the movies cost $0.05 in 1930 and it cost $7.00 in 1990, what was the average increase per year between 1930 and 1990? _____

5. In 1927, Charles Lindbergh flew nonstop from New York to Paris, France, in 33 hours. The distance from New York to Paris is approximately 4,800 miles. Lindbergh was flying at an average speed of _____ miles per hour.

6. In 1996, a jet carrying 400 passengers could fly from New York to Paris in 8 hours. The average speed per hour is _____ .

7. The jet in problem 5 flies to Paris in approximately a) $\frac{1}{8}$ b) $\frac{1}{10}$ c) $\frac{1}{4}$ d) $\frac{1}{5}$ the time it took Lindbergh.

8. Richard E. Byrd was the first to fly over the North Pole on May 4, 1926, and the South Pole on November 28–29, 1929. If each pole is at 90° latitude, what is the total degrees of latitude between the two poles? _____

Name _____ Date _____

United States Map

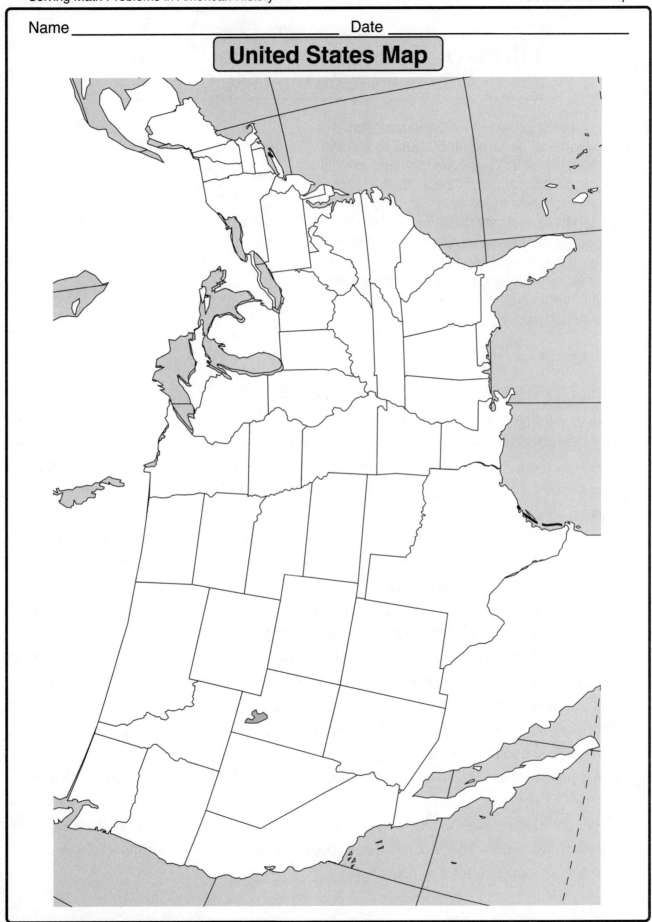

Answer Keys

Exercise 1: Population in Early America (pages 2–3)

	Increase 1660 to 1700		Increase 1700 to 1740		Increase 1740 to 1780	
	Total	Percentage	Total	Percentage	Total	Percentage
CT	18,000	225%	64,000	246%	117,000	130%
DE	2,000	400%	17,500	700%	25,000	125%
GA	******	******	******	******	54,000	2,700%
MD	22,000	275%	86,000	287%	129,000	111%
MA	34,000	155%	96,000	171%	117,000	77%
NH	3,500	232%	18,000	360%	65,000	283%
NJ	******	******	37,000	264%	89,000	175%
NY	14,000	280%	45,000	237%	147,000	230%
NC	10,000	1,000%	41,000	373%	218,000	419%
PA	******	******	68,000	378%	241,000	280%
RI	4,500	300%	19,000	317%	28,000	112%
SC	******	******	39,000	650%	135,000	300%
VA	32,000	119%	121,000	205%	358,000	199%

	Increase 1660 to 1780	
	Total	Percentage
CT	199,000	2,488%
DE	445,000	8,900%
MD	237,000	2,963%
MA	247,000	1,123%
NH	86,500	5,767%
NY	206,000	4,120%
NC	269,000	26,900%
RI	51,500	3,433%
VA	511,000	1,893%

1. North Carolina
2. Virginia
3. Massachusetts
4. Delaware
5. Delaware
6. Massachusetts
7. Virginia
8. Delaware
9. Georgia
10. Massachusetts
11. Virginia
12. Delaware

Exercise 2: Roman Numerals (pages 5–6)
1. MDCCXXXI
2. DVIII
3. CLII
4. CLXII
5. MDCXI
6. MDXII
7. 600
8. 11
9. 63
10. 26
11. 1561
12. 672
13. 900
14. 400
15. 90
16. 404
17. 409
18. 44
19. XXXIV
20. XIX
21. VII
22. 26
23. 162
24. 60
25. 39
26. 27
27. 250
28. XLV
29. LXIX
30. LIV
31. XVII
32. XXIII
33. CCCXVIII
34. CDXC
35. 1,600
36. 1,720
37. 336
38. 1,860
39. 633
40. 1,826
41. 1,512
42. 1,484

Exercise 3: How Many Logs to Build a Cabin? (page 9)
1. 20
2. 20
3. 22
4. 22
5. 22
6. 22
7. 24
8. 24

Exercise 4: How Much Sod Is Needed for a Sod House? (page 11)
1. 133
2. 495
3. 253
4. 158
5. 416

Exercise 5: Figure the Income of a Nineteenth Century Farmer (page 13)
1. $13.36
2. $6.06
3. $65.05
4. $344.63
5. $50.08
6. $501.76
7. $450.73
8. $948.13
9. $355.84
10. $9.12
11. $189.28
12. $119.21
13. $36.74
14. $23.46
15. $9.67
16. $126.54
17. $43.52
18. $3.42
19. $3,184.60

Exercise 6: Find the Gross and Net Weight and Price of Hogs (page 15)

1. 402	11. $2.76
2. 496	12. $3.26
3. 510	13. $5.31
4. 403	14. $3.18
5. 326	15. $5.69
6. 646	16. $3.43
7. 491	17. $3.10
8. 390	18. $5.00
9. 601	19. $5.23
10. 659	20. $5.71

Exercise 7: Figuring the Capacities of Granaries, Bins, and Wagons (page 17)

1. 3,456 cu. ft.
2. 4,928 cu. ft.
3. 8,250 cu. ft.
4. 16,016 cu. ft.
5. 12,558 cu. ft.
6. 2,340 cu. ft.
7. 2,208 cu. ft.
8. 1,680 cu. ft.
9. 1,672 cu. ft.
10. 558 cu. ft.
11. 498 cu. ft.
12. 397 cu. ft.
13. 414 cu. ft.
14. 970 cu. ft.
15. 819 cu. ft.
16. 655 cu. ft.
17. 1,324 cu. ft.
18. 1,234 cu. ft.
19. 105 cu. ft.
20. 123 cu. ft.
21. 197 cu. ft.
22. 70 cu. ft.
23. 80 cu. ft.
24. 294 cu. ft.
25. 238 cu. ft.
26. 288 cu. ft.

Exercise 8: Finding the Weights of Haystacks (page 18)

1. 1,280	~1.83 tons
2. 1,512	~3.02 tons
3. 1,547	~3.09 tons
4. 1,430	~2.04 tons
5. 1,672	~3.34 tons
6. 1,666	~3.33 tons
7. 1,450	~2.07 tons
8. 1,315	~1.88 tons
9. 1,593	~3.18 tons
10. 2,112	~4.22 tons

Exercise 9: Finding the Volumes of Cisterns (page 19)

1. 2,411.52 cu. ft.
2. 2,154.04 cu. ft.
3. 552.64 cu. ft.
4. 1,469.52 cu. ft.
5. 1,387.45 cu. ft.
6. 789.62 cu. ft.
7. 1,694.17 cu. ft.
8. 317.34 cu. ft.
9. 4,695.57 cu. ft.
10. 3,404.53 cu. ft.

Exercise 10: Figuring the Volumes of Barrels (page 22)

1. 1,727 cu. in.
2. 2,462 cu. in.
3. 1,922 cu. in.
4. 4,832 cu. in.
5. 2,904 cu. in.
6. 4,075 cu. in.
7. 2,928 cu. in.
8. 2,686 cu. in.
9. 4,149 cu. in.
10. 6,745 cu. in.

Exercise 11: Figuring the Board Feet in Lumber (page 23)

1. 16 board ft.
2. 17 board ft.
3. 14 board ft.
4. 16 board ft.
5. 31 board ft.
6. 37 board ft.

Exercise 12: Floor, Wall and Ceiling Measurements (pages 24–25)
1. $19.93
2. $20.92
3. $21.15
4. $13.46
5. $16.94
6. $23.94
7. $24.01
8. $16.07
9. $22.26
10. $18.16

Exercise 13: How Many Bricks to Build a House? (page 26–27)
1.   a. 24,300   b. $182.25
2.   a. 193,950   b. $1450.75
3.   a. 94,725   b. $710.44
4.   a. 202,275   b. $1,482.68
5.   a. 45,675   b. $338

Exercise 14: How Many Bricks to Build a Sidewalk (pages 28–29)
1.   a. 240   b. $1.79
2.   a. 844   b. $6.32
3.   a. 2,475   b. $18.54
4.   a. 4,320   b. $32.40
5.   a. 1,620   b. $12.07

Exercise 15: How Many Shingles to Cover a Roof? (page 30)
1. 15,488
2. 16,960
3. 13,110
4. 31,201
5. 29,626
6. 21,854
7. 20,263
8. 11,933
9. 16,423
10. 15,974

Exercise 16: Figuring Ferryboat Income (page 32)
1. $3.13
2. $5.25
3. $3.18
4. $1.79
5. $1.13
6. $4.48
7. $1.28
8. $1.04
9. $0.40
10. $4.11
11. $2.70
12. $3.09
13. $4.68
14. $3.19
15. $7.76
16. $4.42
17. $6.60
18. $25.90
19. $7.44
20. $3.51
21. $4.13
22. $8.69
23. $6.44
24. $0.37
25. $114.71

Exercise 17: Profit or Loss at the General Store (pages 34–35)
1.   a. $0.77   b. $8.45
2.   a. $0.71   b. $7.22
3.   a. $7.50   b. $132.50
4.   a. $19.11   b. $127.89
5.   a. $44.63   b. $569.63
6.   a. $19.62   b. $593.38
7.   a. $0.07/yd.   b. $0.44/yd.
8.   a. $0.03/yd.   b. $0.39/yd.

Exercise 18: Percentages of Profit or Loss (page 36)
1. 6%   5. 21%
2. 17%   6. 8%
3. 24%   7. 23%
4. 13%   8. 12%

Exercise 19: Visiting the General Store (page 38)

Date	Entry	Debit	Credit	Balance
May 29				$37.15
June 10	12 lbs. and 3 oz. of butter at 9 1/2 cents per lb.	$1.16		$38.31
"	3 sacks of coffee weighing 3 1/2 lbs per sack at 12 1/2 cents. per lb.	$1.31		$39.62
"	4.25 doz. eggs at 8 1/2 cts. doz.	$0.36		$39.98
"	125 lbs. sugar at 6 1/4 cts. lb	$7.81		$47.79
"	12 3/4 yds of cloth at 75 cts. yd.	$9.56		$57.35
"	Traded 6 bushels of potatoes at $1.01 per bushel.		$6.06	$51.29
"	Traded 35 bushels of wheat at $1.37 bushel		$47.95	$3.34
Balance				$3.34

Exercise 20: Figuring a Peddler's Inventory (pages 39–40)

1. $17.50
2. $2.34
3. $60.00
4. $0.75
5. $12.80
6. $12.60
7. $82.50
8. $8.16
9. $50.40
10. $37.50
11. $10.00
12. $190.08
13. $37.80
14. $0.90
15. $6.93
16. $1.49
17. $4.50
18. $5.94
19. $1.13
20. $21.25
21. $1.90
22. $10.81
23. $9.00
24. $7.20
25. $37.80
26. $8.88
27. $3.00
28. $19.50
29. $37.80
30. $153.00
31. $3.40
32. $6.72
33. $47.30
34. $0.80
35. $127.50
36. $10.00
37. $39.33
38. $0.46
39. $9.00
40. $14.16
41. $19.69
42. $15.17
43. $6.20
44. $17.08
45. $14.63
46. $0.45
47. $2.16
48. $3.05
49. $6.08
50. $7.70
51. $34.83
52. 30.00
53. $1,269.17

Exercise 21: Completing a Wages Table (page 42)

Weekly Rate		$3.00	$3.50	$4.00	$4.50	$5.00	$5.50	$6.00	$6.50	$7.00	$7.50	$8.00	$9.00	$10.00
Hourly Rate Hours Worked	1	0.05	0.06	0.07	0.08	0.08	0.09	0.10	0.11	0.12	0.13	0.13	0.15	0.17
	2	0.10	0.12	0.13	0.15	0.17	0.18	0.20	0.22	0.23	0.25	0.27	0.30	0.33
	3	0.15	0.17	0.20	0.23	0.25	0.27	0.30	0.32	0.35	0.38	0.40	0.45	0.50
	4	0.20	0.23	0.26	0.30	0.33	0.37	0.40	0.43	0.47	0.50	0.53	0.60	0.67
	5	0.25	0.29	0.33	0.38	0.42	0.46	0.50	0.54	0.58	0.63	0.67	0.75	0.83
	6	0.30	0.35	0.40	0.45	0.50	0.55	0.60	0.65	0.70	0.75	0.80	0.90	1.00
	7	0.35	0.41	0.46	0.53	0.58	0.64	0.70	0.76	0.82	0.88	0.93	1.05	1.17
	8	0.40	0.47	0.53	0.60	0.66	0.73	0.80	0.86	0.93	1.00	1.06	1.20	1.33
	9	0.45	0.53	0.59	0.68	0.75	0.82	0.90	0.97	1.05	1.13	1.20	1.35	1.50
Daily Rate Days Worked	1	0.50	0.58	0.67	0.75	0.83	0.92	1.00	1.08	1.17	1.25	1.33	1.50	1.67
	2	1.00	1.17	1.33	1.50	1.66	1.83	2.00	2.17	2.33	2.50	2.67	3.00	3.33
	3	1.50	1.75	2.00	2.25	2.49	2.75	3.00	3.25	3.50	3.75	4.00	4.50	5.00
	4	2.00	2.33	2.66	3.00	3.32	3.66	4.00	4.33	4.66	5.00	5.33	6.00	6.67
	5	2.50	2.92	3.33	3.75	4.15	4.58	5.00	5.42	5.83	6.25	6.67	7.50	8.33

Exercise 22: Table Showing the Equivalent Decimals of Common Fractions (page 43)

Common Fraction	$\frac{1}{2}$	$\frac{1}{3}$	$\frac{2}{3}$	$\frac{1}{4}$	$\frac{3}{4}$	$\frac{1}{5}$	$\frac{2}{5}$	$\frac{3}{5}$	$\frac{4}{5}$
Decimal Equivalent	0.5	0.33	0.66	0.25	0.75	0.2	0.4	0.6	0.8
Common Fraction	$\frac{1}{6}$	$\frac{5}{6}$	$\frac{1}{8}$	$\frac{3}{8}$	$\frac{5}{8}$	$\frac{7}{8}$	$\frac{1}{12}$	$\frac{5}{12}$	$\frac{7}{12}$
Decimal Equivalent	0.167	0.834	0.125	0.375	0.625	0.875	0.083	0.417	0.583
Common Fraction	$\frac{11}{12}$	$\frac{1}{16}$	$\frac{3}{16}$	$\frac{5}{16}$	$\frac{7}{16}$	$\frac{9}{16}$	$\frac{11}{16}$	$\frac{13}{16}$	$\frac{15}{16}$
Decimal Equivalent	0.917	0.063	0.188	0.313	0.438	0.563	0.688	0.813	0.938

Exercise 23: Slavery Bar Graph (page 45)

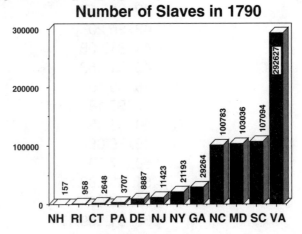

Number of Slaves in 1790

Exercise 24: Slavery Circle Graph (page 46)

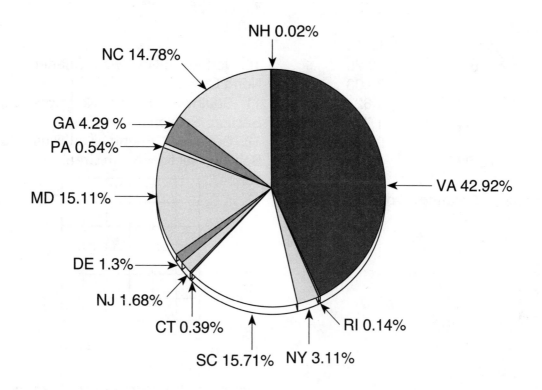

NH 0.02%

NC 14.78%

GA 4.29 %

PA 0.54%

MD 15.11%

DE 1.3%

NJ 1.68%

CT 0.39%

SC 15.71%   NY 3.11%

RI 0.14%

VA 42.92%

Exercise 25: Using Ratios to Compare Slaves to Freedmen (page 48)

Ratio	Decimal Equivalent
1. 1,798:19,829	0.091
2. 2:625	0.003
3. 490,865:58,042	8.457
4. 435,080:2,690	161.740
5. 111,115:144	771.632
6. 61,745:932	66.25
7. 462,198:3,500	132.057
8. 331,726:18,647	17.790
9. 436,631:773	564.853
10. 331,059:30,463	10.868
11. 402,406:9,914	40.590
12. 182,566:355	514.270
13. 225,483:10,684	21.105
14. 87,189:83,942	1.039
15. 275,719:7,300	37.770

Exercise 26: Using Ratios to Compare Farm Sizes (pages 50–51)

1. New York
2. Delaware
3. Pennsylvania
4. Delaware
5. New York
6. Delaware
7. New York
8. Rhode Island
9. New York
10. Rhode Island
11. Virginia
12. Maine
13. Virginia
14. South Carolina

Ratio	Decimal Equivalent
15. 936:39	24
16. 1,719:9	191
17. 2,032:29	70.07
18. 859:45	19.09
19. 261:11	23.73

Ratio	Decimal Equivalent
20. 321:92	3.49
21. 63:14	4.5
22. 1,059:17	62.29
23. 5,232:225	23.25
24. 4,821:61	79.03
25. 2,351:2,882	0.82
26. 2,050:1,184	1.73
27. 352:1,359	0.26
28. 22,056:5,967	3.70

Exercise 27: Reading a Coordinate Graph (page 53)
1. (-4, -2)
2. (+1, +1)
3. (-5, +1)
4. (-1, +2)
5. (-4, +3)
6. (-1, -2)
7. (-2, +4)
8. (+2, +4)
9. (-3, -3)
10. (+3, +1)
11. (-4, +2)
12. (+4,+4)
13. (+1, -1)
14. (-2, -4)
15. (+2, -2)

Exercise 28: Surveying the Land of the Frontier (pages 54–57)
1.

1	2	3	4	5	6
7	8	9	10	11	12
13	14	15	16	17	18
19	20	21	22	23	24
25	26	27	28	29	30
31	32	33	34	35	36

2. a. 36; b. sections; c. 36; d. 1; e. 1
3. 640
4. 160
5. Because each small square is one-fourth of a section.

6. a. D; b. C; c. B; d. A
7. Teacher check
8. 160
9. 40
10. Northeast; Northwest Quarter; Section; North Creek
11. Southwest Fourth; Northwest Quarter Section; Section; North Creek
12. Southeast Fourth; Northwest Quarter Section; Section; North Creek
13–14.

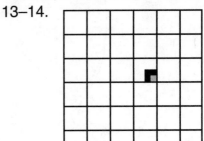

15. 40
16. 120

Exercise 29: Comparing Farming and Nonfarming Populations (page 58)
1. 4,550,000
2. 29,400,000
3. 30,000,000
4. 38,000,000
5. 7,500,000
6. Teacher check
7. Answers will vary but should include the following information:
The percent of population living on farms decreased from 1860 to 1990, and the trend is likely to continue to 2010.

Exercise 30: Pie Graphs and Population (page 59)
1. 65%
2. 3%
3. 4,550,000
4. shaded
5. 8,280,000
6. shaded

Exercise 31: Ratios and Population (page 60)

1. $\frac{5}{7}$
2. $\frac{9}{14}$
3. $\frac{1}{4}$
4. $\frac{1}{5}$
5. $\frac{1}{40}$
6. 7
7. 70
8. 120
9. 200
10. 240
11. decreasing; increasing

Exercise 32: The Law of Supply (page 61)

1. 20
2. 40
3. 70
4–5. Teacher check

Exercise 33: The Law of Demand (page 62)

1. $2.50
2. $1.75
3. $1.25
4. Decreases
5. Demand
6. Increases
7. Demand

Exercise 34: Supply and Demand for Wheat (pages 63–64)

1. $0.50
2. $500.00
3. Teacher check
4. 4,000
5. $2,000.00
6. $500.00
7. $60.00
8. $60.00; $560.00
9. $30.00; $530.00
10. $440.00
11–13. Teacher check

Exercise 35: Inflation and Corn Production (page 65)

1. $0.05
2. a) 2
3. $0.11
4. a) 4
5. 5%
6. Increased
7–8. Teacher check

Exercise 36: Helpful Farming Inventions (pages 66–67)

1. Burbank
2. Contour farming
3. Carleton
4. Crop rotation
5. Tractor
6. Reaper
7. Truck
8. Whitney
9. Dry farming
10. Plow

Exercise 37: Water Transportation (page 68)

Teacher check map

Exercise 38: Railroad Transportation (page 69)

1. b
2. d
3. a. $\frac{1}{4}$ b. 25%
4. a. 4 b. 400%
5. a. 1.075 b. 107.5%
6. a. $\frac{32}{43}$ b. 74%

Exercise 39: Railroad Transportation Map Activity (page 70)

Teacher check map
1. Minnesota, North Dakota, Montana, Idaho, Washington
2. Iowa, Nebraska, Wyoming, Utah, Nevada, California
3. Missouri, Kansas, New Mexico, Arizona, Colorado, California
4. Washington, Oregon, California

Exercise 40: U.S. Highway System Map Activity (page 71)
Teacher check map
1. Harrisburg, Columbus, Indianapolis, St. Louis, Kansas City, Denver
2. Columbia, Augusta, Atlanta, Birmingham, Jackson, Shreveport, Dallas, Ft. Worth
3. Highway 25
4. 76, 25, 70
5. Highway 94
6. Highway 5

Exercise 41: Comparing Modes of Transportation (page 72)
1. 120
2. 4
3. 1.2
4. 46.67 hours
5a. rivers/lakes
   b. lakes/rivers
   c. railroads
   d. automobile
   e. highway
6. Teacher check

Exercise 42: The Iron/Steel Industry Develops (pages 73–74)
1–4. Teacher check map
5. Teacher check
6. c
7. a
8. b

Exercise 43: The Growth of Labor Unions (page 76)
1. 500,000   5. 20,000,000
2. 3,500,000   6. 16,500,000
3. 8,500,000   7. 13,500,000
4. 17,000,000   8. 1940–1960

Exercise 44: Boom and Bust in the American Economy (page 77)
All the items should have a plus sign since they all contributed to the Great Depression.

Exercise 45: Learning About the 1920s and 1930s Matching Activity (pages 78–80)
1. CC   17. K
2. F   18. FF
3. E   19. D
4. EE   20. R
5. Z   21. W
6. AA   22. S
7. J   23. A
8. O   24. U
9. BB   25. DD
10. L   26. G
11. B   27. N
12. M   28. Q
13. P   29. X
14. V   30. Y
15. I   31. T
16. H   32. C

Exercise 46: Entertainment and Heroes of the 1920s and 1930s (page 81)
1. b
2a. 282   b. 56.4
3. a
4. ~$0.12 per year
5. 145
6. 600 mph
7. c
8. 180°